GOD'S PROPHET, GOD'S SERVANT

A Study in Jeremiah
and Isaiah 40-55

JOHN GOLDINGAY

WIPF & STOCK · Eugene, Oregon

Wipf and Stock Publishers
199 W 8th Ave, Suite 3
Eugene, OR 97401

God's Prophet, God's Servant
A Study in Jeremiah and Isaiah 40-55
By Goldingay, John
Copyright © 1994 by Goldingay, John All rights reserved.
Softcover ISBN-13: 979-8-3852-3234-5
Hardcover ISBN-13: 979-8-3852-3235-2
eBook ISBN-13: 979-8-3852-3236-9
Publication date 9/9/2024
Previously published by Clements Publishing, 1994

*In memory of my
father and mother*

Contents

Foreword 5
Introduction 7

PART ONE
Jeremiah: "A burning fire in my heart"

1. What being a prophet costs 17
2. Who a prophet is identified with 35
3. What distinguishes a prophet 49
4. What makes someone a prophet? 65
5. The moment of fulfillment 75

PART TWO
Isaiah 40–55: "A light to the nations"

6. The chosen servant (Isaiah 41:1–20) 87
7. The faithful servant (Isaiah 41:21–42:17) 101
8. The blind servant (Isaiah 42:18–48:22) 115
9. The persistent servant (Isaiah 49–50) 133
10. The triumphant servant (Isaiah 52:13–53:12) 149

Foreword

These studies of Jeremiah and Isaiah 40–55 arose from my teaching and preaching in Britain, whose contexts I am glad to recall: especially the congregation of Christ Church, Chilwell, Nottingham, the summer house party of the Church's Ministry among the Jews at High Leigh, Hoddesdon, and most of all the students, faculty, and staff of St John's College, Nottingham. I am grateful to Patti Boyland and Janet Gillard for their original typing from my much-emended handwriting. The first edition was published by Paternoster Press in 1984 and reprinted in 1994. In connection with this revised edition, I am grateful to Alex Pak of the Faculty Publications Office at Fuller Theological Seminary, Pasadena, California, for scanning the original volume, and to an Irish American friend, Una Lucey, for trying to persuade me to write better English. I suspect the language is now a mixture of British and American, but that is the language I speak. I have rewritten the text (e.g., to inclusivize the language), but not altered the substance very much. If I were writing on Isaiah 53 today, I would handle the detail of that chapter differently at many points, but this would not make a significant difference to the thrust of my exposition.

I have occasionally explicitly quoted from works on these two prophets, or on the Old Testament more generally, and I am, of course, much more indebted to such works than a mere occasional quotation may suggest. The reader who wants to study these prophets further might try some of these works but there are more recent short commentaries on Isaiah by John Sawyer and on Jeremiah by Robert Davidson in the Daily Study Bible series (St Andrew's Press, Edinburgh, and WJK, Louisville). Good fuller commentaries are Claus Westermann's *Isaiah 40–66* (SCM, London, and WJK, Louisville) and Walter Brueggemann's *Jeremiah* (Eerdmans, Grand Rapids and Cambridge, UK). I have now written the commentary on Isaiah in the New International Biblical Commentary series (Paternoster, Carlisle and Hendrickson, Peabody, MA) and hope to publish more detailed works on Isaiah 40–55 in 2002.

For quotations from the Bible, I have occasionally quoted from some of the standard translations, the RSV (Revised Standard Version), NRSV (New Revised Standard Version), JB (Jerusalem Bible), NEB (New English Bible), and GNB (Good News Bible: Today's English Version). I am glad to acknowledge the use of these. Often they vary from each other, however (and commentaries on the books extend the range of possible interpretations of passages). I have had to come to my own conclusions at such points, and in the pages that follow I have therefore usually provided my own translation though I have not neglected to adopt happy renderings of particular phrases from the standard versions.

—John Goldingay

Introduction

The Bible begins with an epic story of some quarter of a million words. This story opens in Genesis with the creating of order, meaning, and life out of formlessness, emptiness, and nothingness. It closes in 2 Kings with order, meaning, and life disappearing into formlessness, emptiness, and nothingness. The independent existence of the Judean nation collapses with an air of finality as its land is invaded and despoiled, its cities and central shrine are devastated, and its leadership is transported in chains to Babylon.

The affliction of the people in this period of defeat and exile is mirrored in the story of the prophet Jeremiah (who went through the years leading up to exile with his people). It is also mirrored in the portrayal of the enigmatic servant figure(s) of whom we read in Isaiah 40–55. But the affliction of Judah and the affliction of the prophet or the servant are not identical in significance. The suffering of the nation as a whole is seen (in these prophetic books and elsewhere) as the deserved punishment of the unfaithfulness to God and injustice among human beings that characterized the nation. But the affliction of

Jeremiah and the servant is unmerited. Strikingly, the moment of deserved punishment is also the occasion that raises the question of undeserved suffering as sharply as any period of Old Testament history did.

Jeremiah and Isaiah 40–55 tackle this problem as an urgent challenge to practical theology, not as an exercise in philosophical theology in an abstract sense. They are concerned with the existential question of finding meaning in affliction. Why does being a prophet involve the experiences it does? How does a prophet know that the word that costs so much really comes from God? How can a prophet remain faithful to a calling amidst all the pressures to abandon it? These are some of Jeremiah's questions. They are taken further in the servant prophecies of Isaiah 40–55, where there is the most profound realization in the Old Testament of what must be involved in being God's servant if that calling is to achieve his deepest purpose.

The questions taken up by these two books are perennial ones. The vision of "the servant church" is one that ever confronts Christians with a challenge that seems at point after point way beyond anything we have yet taken seriously. For the calling of the servant was not intended to be something meant only for the Jeremiahs or the Jesuses of this world. It was simply what was involved in being the people of God. It was, one might say, a very democratic notion.

Nor is the world inclined to be patient of prophets if they fulfill their calling and say the straightest things even to those in the highest power. The church, too, is often impatient of prophets, particularly when it is on the verge or in the midst of the exile experience-enfeebled, discredited, defeated, demoralized. So people whose only purpose is to get the church to face the truth ought not to be surprised if they are made to feel rather like Jeremiah.

His self-portrait thus issues its challenges to Christian believers in general, though in particular to two archetypal kinds of believers. The first are people who are triumphant in their

Introduction

Christian living and their Christian service, people to whom God always seem to be real, who are always full of God's praise, who seem to be followed by blessing wherever they go. They are Christians who are triumphant, and in danger of being triumphalist. Jeremiah reminds us, as does Paul centuries later, that triumph and affliction usually go together in the faith of the Bible. Triumph, blessing, and praise are most authentic when there is a cross at the heart of them. Jeremiah is a man who before Christ embodies a saying of Christ: "If anyone would come after me, *let them deny themselves and take up their cross and follow me*" (Mark 8:34). The glory of God and the triumph of God tend to be tied up with crosses. There is a contrast here with the glib promises that sometimes characterize the preaching of the gospel, the easy offers of freedom, harmony, and joy available in Christ to the bound, the broken, and the joyless. Christ also brings a cross, and a cross itself means disharmony. It means not peace, but a sword. That is how it was for Jeremiah.

But Jeremiah's story also illustrates a converse truth, and here it speaks to the opposite kind of person. These are people who find that the parts of the Bible they can easily identify with and find themselves in are the parts that talk about doubt, affliction, and protest, that speak of the difficulty of believing and of the implausibility of the faith. In recent decades, for instance, there has been an increased interest in scholarly circles in the wisdom books of the Old Testament, and part of the reason for this is that here, in Job and Ecclesiastes, it is people's doubts and protests that are the books' point of departure. Bishop Stuart Blanch *begins* his book on the Old Testament, *For All Mankind*, with Ecclesiastes. In Paul, too, many people find themselves able to identify with the experience of 2 Corinthians at least as readily as with that of Romans or 1 Corinthians. Among the prophets it is Jeremiah, or his spiritual grandfather Hosea, who represents this message. He is quite open about his protests, his questions, his affliction, and his doubts. He admits when he is defeated, though he is not in the end defeatist.

Here, in fact, is the lesson on which he offers so much insight: how to be triumphant without being triumphalist, and how to be defeated without being defeatist. He shows us, in fact, that the key lies in relating these two experiences, triumph and defeat, to each other. We have *treasure*, but in *clay jars*:

> Always carrying in the body the death of Jesus, so that the life of Jesus may also be made visible in our bodies.... We are always being given up to death for Jesus' sake, so that the life of Jesus may be made visible in our mortal flesh. (2 Cor. 4:7,10,11 NRSV)

The prophet and the servant suggest to us what it means to have treasure in earthen vessels.

But before we go on to look at the books of Jeremiah and Isaiah, some comments need to be made concerning the origin of the material we shall be considering. A look through a few pages of the book of Jeremiah soon makes clear that much of the material is not Jeremiah's poems or sermons but stories about Jeremiah, or about events in his time (see, for instance, chs 37–44). These stories about Jeremiah were apparently collected after the fall of Jerusalem by Judeans who now saw that he had been right, and that it was therefore important to understand what he had been doing. They collected his teaching so that they and their contemporaries could take it more seriously than it had been taken before the exile. Thus they were not concerned merely to preserve the message of Jeremiah out of an antiquarian interest in the past. They wanted to bring a message to the present, to the time of exile in which they themselves lived. They wanted to apply Jeremiah's teaching to their own day, because they believed it was God's word and had a message for them.

This introduces a complication for us. How far are they relating to us exactly what Jeremiah said; how far are they applying his message to their own age? There seems little reason to question whether the passages printed as poetry in modern Bibles go back to Jeremiah himself. The passages printed in

Introduction

ordinary prose, however, may well be later preachers' sermons preached on texts from Jeremiah's words, or may be what these preachers in the exile believed needed to be said in their day to continue Jeremiah's ministry. Some of what we have in the book of Jeremiah, then, is not what Jeremiah actually was and said in his own day. It is what he meant to people who lived in the exile, who now wanted to help people see that he had spoken the word of Yahweh and must still be listened to.

If this is right, then the book called Jeremiah is not a contemporary photograph of the prophet, but a later portrait of him—or rather, contemporary records (the poetry) are set in the context of later perspective (the prose). And overall, we are enriched. In the chapters that follow, I shall not be trying to isolate the contemporary record from the later perspective, but reading the material as it stands as the account of what Jeremiah meant to those who looked back on his ministry.

When we move on to consider the motif of the servant in Isaiah 40–55, a related issue arises. Here is the message of the book called Isaiah to the people of Judah in exile in the sixth century BC. But the prophet Isaiah lived in the eighth century BC. How did there come to be so many chapters of prophecies to the people in exile, in a book that begins two hundred years previously? There are two main possible answers. One is that, despite the difference in date, all sixty-six chapters in the book came from the prophet Isaiah whose name appears at the beginning of it. On this view, since God *could* have revealed this message to Isaiah, there is no reason not to take the book at its face value; we may assume that God *did* reveal to Isaiah the message destined for those who would be in exile much later. The other approach is to assume that the book as a whole is more of an anthology than this first view implies. The work began as the ministry of Isaiah, but prophets who brought God's word to subsequent periods added later messages to his. There are links between the different parts of the book (for instance, a favorite title for God throughout is the phrase "the holy one of Israel"). These may suggest that the authors of the later prophecies believed that God had given them the mantle that Isaiah once wore, as Elisha had literally worn the mantle of Elijah (2 Kings 1).

I myself think that, while God *could* indeed have revealed the messages in Isaiah 40–55 two centuries before the exile, it is difficult to see why God *would* have done so. They were irrelevant to the eighth century and God speaks as if directly addressing the exiles, not as if addressing their ancestors. So I assume that they are the words of a prophet who lived in Babylon during the exile. I shall refer to the author as "the prophet" or as "the Isaiah of the exile" or as "Second Isaiah"— because this prophet does seem to be seeking to bring to a new day the message that Isaiah would have brought had he still been alive.

It may be that the reader finds it difficult to accept these approaches to the origin of the material in Jeremiah and Isaiah 40–55. If so, it may be worth noting that it makes little difference to the meaning of the books: Cyrus the Persian is Cyrus the Persian living in the time of the exile, whenever the book was written.

PART ONE

Jeremiah

"It is like a burning fire in my heart"
(Jeremiah 20:9)

CHAPTER ONE

What being a prophet costs

So Jeremiah is the 2 Corinthians of the Old Testament. Now I have read somewhere that in the New Testament there is a suggestive sequence in the way Romans, 1 Corinthians, and 2 Corinthians follow each other. When the gospel of grace is boldly preached, as it is in Romans, it will cause a revolution whose spin-off may be the troubles reflected in 1 Corinthians. Then, dealing with these traumas may well cost the preacher personally, as 2 Corinthians shows it cost Paul.

In the Old Testament, Isaiah 1–39 might be seen as an equivalent to Romans. Here the election love of God is clearly declared. Despite the sin of Judah, God will keep the promise to David. God will not let Jerusalem fall. This promise of God's grace is only too enthusiastically received and Judah gains new confidence in God's irrevocable commitment to it. But when God makes a commitment like that, expectations from God come with it. Judah becomes deaf to the note in its faith that spoke of these expectations. Thus through subsequent prophets, including Jeremiah, there run indictment after indictment of the wantonness of the people: of their moral laxity, their broken relationships, their social disorder, their faithless worship, their twisted theology. The charges are quite parallel to those of 1 Corinthians. But interwoven with these indictments in Jeremiah is the other note to which we have drawn attention, the record of the struggles and affliction of the prophet himself. Dealing with the troubles of Judah brought its personal cost to Jeremiah. Here is the Paul of 2 Corinthians, as it were.

Jeremiah unveils his own experience of being continually given up to death, his own proving of what being a prophet costs, in a series of prayers and protests that are grouped together in chapters 11–20 of his book. These poems are often referred to as the "confessions" of Jeremiah, but this is a misleading description. They are not passages in which Jeremiah is confessing his sin, or even, generally, confessing the greatness of God. They are the lamentations of Jeremiah. As far as their form goes, they are like the laments in the Psalter, in which believers pour out their suffering, their anger, and their longings to God.

They come quite early in Jeremiah's book, and it has often been inferred that they thus belong to a relatively early stage in his ministry—that they record the spiritual crisis he experienced at that point as he wrestled with the cost of being a prophet. On this view, it was a crisis he came through triumphantly. Later in the book, we see Jeremiah confronting Jehoiakim and Hananiah and Zedekiah, we see him hauled before the temple authorities and put in the stocks (ch. 20), threatened with the death sentence (ch. 26), and imprisoned in the court of the guard (ch. 32). We see him dying of hunger in a disused water cistern (ch. 38), bound in chains by the Babylonians (ch. 40), ridiculed by Hananiah (ch. 28), ignored by Jehoiakim (ch. 36), and contradicted by Azariah (ch. 43). When we see him *outwardly* afflicted, do we see nevertheless a man who had already walked through the fires and come out the other side, who now through it all stands confident, firm, unwavering and resolute—inner doubt resolved, strength of faith now triumphant?

In subsequent chapters, Jeremiah is indeed outwardly unwavering and resolute. But I wonder if we are to assume that

What being a prophet costs

he had long ago won the final victory over his inner turmoil and was never any more tempted to give up in despair. The mere fact that the laments are collected in chapters 11–20 does not entitle us to make the assumption that inner turmoil belonged to only one chronological period. While these chapters do major on his inner suffering while chapters 26–45 concentrate on his outward affliction, the Book of Jeremiah is not arranged chronologically, and I suspect that these are two aspects of his continuing prophetic calling. This double experience, of inner suffering and outward affliction, characterized his ministry all through.

Perhaps the very fact that the last of the confessions in chapter 20 (last, that is, in the arrangement of the book) closes with despair and not confidence warns against our understanding these passages as reflecting an admittedly deep but essentially passing spiritual turmoil. And what was true of the inward affliction, that it ends on a down note, ends in turmoil, is true also of the outward suffering. Of course, Jeremiah does have his good moments. In a paradoxical way the fall of Jerusalem is one because that is the point at which he is proved right, when it is established that God has not been fooling him. But even then his message is not taken to heart, and the man who had been dragged by his heels into Jerusalem at the beginning of his ministry (ch. 1) is now dragged by his heels out of Jerusalem at the end of his ministry. He is taken as a lucky charm by Judeans who have decided that the only future lies in refuge in Egypt (ch. 43). As Gerhard von Rad points out in his *Old Testament Theology* (Volume 2, p. 207), no ravens feed Jeremiah as they fed Elijah. No angel stops the lion's mouth for him as one did for Daniel. So almost our last sight of Jeremiah is his back as he turns his feet wearily south, his ministry apparently fruitless, his future apparently only death, far away from the inheritance that he had promised that he and his brethren would repossess in the land (chs 32–33). The story of his outward suffering, like that of his inward affliction, ends in misery. In various ways, then, Jeremiah had to pay the cost of being a prophet.

To stand alone

One element in that cost is that Jeremiah has to be willing to stand alone, to cope with isolation, opposition, betrayal, and attack, even from those who ought to be most loyal to him. Chapter 11 begins with the notes of a sermon by Jeremiah in which he calls on Judah to take seriously the covenant (the solemnly agreed mutual commitment) between itself and Yahweh. But as the sermon notes develop they make it clear that, as far as Jeremiah can see, there is no prospect of that challenge being met. This generation, like previous generations, is totally unresponsive to God, is beyond praying for, and is destined for terrible trouble.

> The word that came to Jeremiah from Yahweh. "Speak to the people who live in Judah and Jerusalem. Say to them, Yahweh, the God of Israel says: 'A curse rests on everyone who does not obey these terms of the covenant that I issued to your ancestors at the time when I brought them out of Egypt, out of the smelting furnace'. I said, 'Listen to my voice and act in accordance with everything that I tell you. You will be my people and I myself will be your God. This will lead to my keeping the oath that I swore to your ancestors, that I would give them a land where milk and honey flow'—as they now have." I answered, "I will, Yahweh" (11:1-5).

The chapter begins uncontroversially enough; it is very reminiscent of the warnings of Deuteronomy 27. But it goes on,

> Then Yahweh said to me, "Proclaim all these things in the cities of Judah and the streets of Jerusalem: Listen to these terms of the covenant and act on them, because I solemnly charged your ancestors at the time when I brought them up from Egypt, and I have continued to do so until today. I have gone out of my way to charge them to listen to my voice. But they did not listen. They did not give me their attention; to a person they lived in accordance with their stubborn, evil inclinations. So I

brought on them all the sanctions of the covenant; I had issued it for them to act on, and they had not" (11:6-8).

The polemic is beginning. Jeremiah declares that the demand of obedience was never met. The nation to a person behaved in a way contrary to Yahweh's will. This claim about the past presages what is to follow about the present generation:

> Then Yahweh said to me, "A conspiracy has emerged among the people who live in Judah and Jerusalem. They have gone back to the perverse ways of their earliest ancestors, who refused to listen to my words. They have followed the worship of other gods. Israel and Judah have broken the covenant I made with their ancestors. This is what Yahweh therefore says: "I am now going to bring upon them a disaster that they will not be able to evade. They can cry out to me but I will not listen to them. The cities of Judah and the inhabitants of Jerusalem can go and cry to the gods to whom they offer up sacrifices, though they will certainly not save them in the hour of disaster. You, Judah, have a god for every city, and in every street of Jerusalem you have put an altar for shame itself, an altar for offering up sacrifices to Baal'" (11:9-13).

Resistance characterizes the present generation as much as it has previous ones. It runs so deep it cannot be undone, nor its punishment averted.

> "So you yourself may not pray for this people. Raise no cries or prayers for it. I shall not be listening when they call on me in their hour of disaster. What place has my beloved in my house, with her devices? Can vows and consecrated meat remove the evil from her? Then you could be jubilant! 'A beautiful, verdant olive-tree with lovely fruit', Yahweh described you. With a roar like thunder he will set fire to it, and its branches will break. The Almighty Yahweh who planted you has threatened you with disaster because of the wrong that Israel and Judah themselves have done. They have made me angry by burning offerings to Baal" (11:14-17).

It is difficult to imagine a more swingeing or unequivocal condemnation of his people than Jeremiah delivers here. Now for Jeremiah to speak like this in the temple could only place him in great danger. Jeremiah's sermon constituted a threatening challenge to both church and state (Israel's glory and its perennial problem was that both were the same). All the vested interests would instinctively combine to crush his message. That was quite obvious—though to Jeremiah, obvious only with hindsight.

> It was Yahweh who made it known to me, thus I knew. At that time you opened my eyes to what they had done. But I was like a pet lamb being taken to the butcher's—I did not know that they were hatching plots against me (11:18-19).

"They" are the people of Anathoth (11:21), Jeremiah's home village, an hour's walk from Jerusalem. Jeremiah perhaps naively hoped that his message would be listened to, that at least his own villagers might be expected to be on his side. But their own countries tend to be the last places that show honor to prophets.

> Let's destroy the tree as well as its fruit (11:19).

Let's make sure, in other words, that it produces nothing else like what we've been hearing.

> Let's cut him off from the land of the living...

We have some vivid verbs in English to make the point: he must be eliminated, exterminated, annihilated.

> ...so that his name will not be remembered any more.

Old Testament believers were granted only a rather vague understanding of life after death (perhaps because the resurrection of the dead would be possible only when Christ had died and been raised as the first fruits of that general resurrection) and thus they valued other assurances that physical death was not the complete end of them. One of these was the realization that their name lived on in the name and in the memory of their descendants. But Jeremiah's attackers want to deprive him even of that.

God's response to all this is twofold. One element in it is to declare that the people of Anathoth will not get away with it. God, too, can use those verbs: Jeremiah's attackers will be eliminated (11:22-23). Jeremiah's prayer for vengeance (11:20) will be answered. But not yet: for the other element in God's response to Jeremiah is less comforting. Jeremiah will have to put up with people like these opponents throughout his ministry. "You'll just have to get a grip, Jeremiah, because things are going to get worse before they get better."

> If you raced with human beings on foot, and they have
> wearied you, how will you get on against horses? (12:5).

"Jeremiah, have you heard of giving people handicaps in a race? Well, you are entered for a race like that. You are running, they are in chariots. Ready, steady, go!" Or, to put it another way, "Jeremiah, you cannot afford to relax even in what looks like easy country. Even in a land of peace where things ought to be safe, you've got to learn to be on your guard, because you have to go through territory that's more like the wild undergrowth along the Jordan, where a snake may be curled under a leaf or a lion be lurking behind the next tree. You've got to learn to be on your guard" (cf 12:5b). There are no lions in the country now, but in those days, down by the Jordan you had to be on your guard. And Jeremiah has to learn to live that way even in territory that looks safe.

> Because even your brothers and your father's house,
> even they have betrayed you.
> Even they are in full cry behind you.
> Do not believe them,
> even though they speak nice words to you (12:6).

A prophet has no honor in his own country *and among his own kin and in his own house* (Mark 6:4). In fact, a prophet has to be willing to stand alone.

To have no private life

Another element in the cost of being a prophet, for Jeremiah, was to have no private life. He had no freedom to make his own decisions about how he lived his life; indeed he was forbidden the life of a normal human being. He had already lost the family in which he was brought up: *Your brothers and your father's house... are in full cry behind you* (12:6). He is allowed no other family to replace that: *You are not to take a wife, nor are you to have sons or daughters in this place* (16:2).

Now normally even people who have no family have their place in the wider community. When occasions of grief or celebration come, they join in these. But this, too, is forbidden to Jeremiah. No rejoicing with those who rejoice, no weeping with those who weep (16:5,8). Jeremiah had to be a man apart. He was denied these normal human experiences.

It was not because Jeremiah was gay that he did not marry, nor was it because he was a loner that he cut himself off from fasting and feasting. It was because this was part of God's calling. His very life was to be part of his preaching. In a sense, of course, it always is. But it was so in a special sense with Jeremiah at this point. "Jeremiah, *why* don't you get married?" (It was a very unusual decision for a man to take in Israel; indeed the married majority still suspects the unmarried minority). "Because Jerusalem at this point of time is no place to be setting up family, no place to be bringing up children."

> For this is Yahweh's message concerning the sons and daughters born in this place, the mothers who bear them and the fathers who beget them in this land. They will die of terrible afflictions, and not be lamented or buried. They will be manure spread on the ground. They will meet their end by sword and by famine, and their corpses will be food for the birds of the air and the animals on the ground (16:3-4).

So the prophet's action was part of his message.

Again, "Why doesn't Jeremiah join with those who mourn—

What being a prophet costs

has he no feelings?" "Because the suffering that is to be experienced here in Jerusalem is so terrible that there will be no comfort; indeed there will be no-one left to mourn."

> High and low in this land will die. They will not be buried, or lamented. No-one will gash themselves or shave their head for them. No one will break mourning bread to comfort someone bereaved, or give them the cup of comfort for their father and mother (16:6-7).

"I am having no sorrowing here, I am withdrawing all consolation, I am refusing all comfort, because of the state of this people."

"And why doesn't Jeremiah join in the celebration of weddings and anniversaries and birthdays?" Because the impending doom of Jerusalem makes celebration grotesque.

> For this is the message of Almighty Yahweh, the God of Israel: "Now, before your own eyes and in your own times I am putting an end to the sound of joy and gladness, the voice of groom and bride, in this place" (16:9).

Jeremiah's personal life helps to make the point. He cannot take a person's normal place in the people's life since God's purpose requires something different. He can show no natural feelings; if he wishes to sorrow with someone he cannot; he cannot marry. He is God's servant, and being a servant means having no feelings of his own or desires of his own. It means being completely at God's disposal in the totality of his private life. Jeremiah reminds us of Hosea, who was told to marry a woman who would turn out to be unfaithful to him, or of Ezekiel, who was told not to mourn his wife when she died. Alongside these we may set the prohibition on Jeremiah's marrying at all. The demand of God for a devotion that expresses itself in total obedience may mean one has no private life. In a sense one has no basic human rights at all.

To be as hard as a rock outside even while you are being torn apart inside

> Jeremiah took his stand in the court of Yahweh's house and said to all the people: These are the words of Almighty Yahweh, the God of Israel: "I am going to bring on this city and on all its cities all the trouble that I have spoken of, because they have resolutely refused to listen to my words." Pashhur the priest, the son of Immer, who was in supreme authority in Yahweh's house, heard Jeremiah prophesying these things. Pashhur had Jeremiah the prophet flogged and put in the stocks at the upper Benjamin Gate of Yahweh's house. Next day Pashhur released Jeremiah from the stocks. Jeremiah then said to him:
> Pashhur is not the name Yahweh has given you, but rather Magor-missabib, Terror-on-all-sides. For these are Yahweh's words: "I am going to make you a terror to yourself and to all your friends. They will fall by the sword of their enemies before your very eyes. I shall give the whole of Judah into the power of the king of Babylon. He will take some into exile in Babylon and put others to the sword. I shall hand over to their enemies all this city's resources, all its gains, all its treasures, all the wealth of the kings of Judah. They will seize them as loot and take them to Babylon. And you yourself, Pashhur, you and all your household, will go into captivity. To Babylon you will go, there you will die, and there you will be buried, you and all your friends to whom you have prophesied lies" (19:14b–20:6).

Despite the treatment he receives from the temple authorities, Jeremiah here appears as a man who can be hard as a rock when he is under huge pressure to change his stance and modify his message. Jeremiah is quite resolute. Yet immediately afterwards (in the arrangement of the material in the book of Jeremiah) we find the forthright prophet suddenly on his knees in despair. It was despite himself that he became a prophet, and (in the light of experiences such as this one) it is despite himself that he remains one. He protests not merely about human opposition but about the divine force that is used against him.

What being a prophet costs

> You used your persuasion, Yahweh, and I was persuaded; you were too strong for me and you overcame me. I am an object of derision all the time. All of them laugh at me, because whenever I speak, I cry for help: "Violence," "outrage," I declare, because Yahweh's word has come to mean scorn and ridicule for me all the time (20:7-8).

Jeremiah was called to be a prophet in 626 BC, and from that point began to declare the message about disaster expressed above in his words to Pashhur. But decades pass and the disaster never arrives. The city remains in one piece. Jeremiah is still prophesying, but he has lost credibility; he has become a figure of fun. Underneath the mocking there may still be some fear, lest Jeremiah should turn out to be right after all (perhaps Pashhur's attempt to silence him implies as much). But he is nevertheless a public laughing stock. He has to declare a message that never seems to come true. *They say to me, "Where is Yahweh's word? Let it come true, if it can!"* (17:15). "Come on, Jeremiah, all these gloomy words about the collapse of the state, about God bringing disaster upon the nation. Come on, let's see it happen then. Fine words of yours, Jeremiah, but they don't come true. Where is Yahweh's word? Let it come true, if it can!" Being a servant of God here involves being apparently abandoned and made a fool of both by human beings and by God.

So what should Jeremiah do? Obviously, he should pack up his scroll and go home. But that is just what he cannot do.

> If I say I will put him out of my mind, I will not speak in his name any more, then it is like a burning fire in my heart, imprisoned within my body. I weary myself holding on to it, and I cannot do so (20:9).

The fire of the wrath of God burns inside him and has to find expression. God not only browbeat him into becoming a prophet in the first place (20:7), but allows him no escape now. God has him and will not let him go. "The cosmic sadist, who plays with me as his pawn, requires me to warn people about a calamity that isn't going to happen, and gives me no choice but to co-operate. Catch 22."

"I have no choice" is clearly very negative. But in another sense it may have a positive implication. Jeremiah has, at least in theory, decided to try turning his back on God and on his calling. But he has found that he cannot. He is a man in a dark room who has found the door, and discovered that it is locked on the other side. So at least he knows where he is, and the purpose of it all may seem mysterious, but the possibility that there is a meaningful purpose is not decreased by his discovery. Indeed, it is increased.

Von Rad summarizes Jeremiah's position in these words:

> The picture we see is of a man appointed to hear the word of God. As a result of this divine call he surrenders much of his freedom—occasionally he is completely overwhelmed by an external compulsion: but paradoxically, just because he has received this call he is able to enjoy an entirely new kind of freedom. Drawn into ever more and more close converse with God, he is privy to the divine purposes and is thereby given the authority to enter into a unique kind of converse with men. The man reflected here is not, of course, an integrated personality. He is divided and sorely troubled as God hides himself from him more and more. Yet, as the martyrdom of Jeremiah testifies, he is in some mysterious way free to choose suffering and so to stand up to God's test (*Old Testament Theology*, Volume 2, p. 76).

In an article on "The Theological Significance of Doubt in the Old Testament" (*Annual of the Swedish Theological Institute* 7, 1968-9, p. 47), Robert Davidson put Jeremiah's position more briefly in the question, "If he had never said 'I'll forget him' would he ever have affirmed so positively 'I can't'?"

So Jeremiah, though outwardly resolute, is inwardly torn apart by humiliation. He is also torn apart by fear. Here we return to the note that appeared in chapter 11.

What being a prophet costs

> I have heard many people whispering—
> There is terror on all sides.
> "Report him, let's report him!"
> All my friends are watching for my downfall.
> "Perhaps he can be persuaded and prevailed over,
> then we can catch him and take vengeance on him" (20:10).

Jeremiah is terrified of the danger he is in at the hand of those who have turned against him. The pressure is real, though it makes one ask whether he has forgotten about Yahweh, forgotten indeed the words he himself wrote a few pages ago:

> Happy the people who trust in Yahweh,
> whose trust is Yahweh.
> They are like a tree planted by water,
> sending out its roots by a stream.
> It is not afraid when hot weather comes.
> Its leaves stay green. In a year of drought it is not anxious,
> it does not stop producing fruit (17:7-8).

Jeremiah has not, in fact, forgotten those declarations of faith. The kind of prayer that Jeremiah has been praying appears also in the psalms, and there it characteristically leads to an expression of confidence in and praise to the God who does answer prayer. The psalmists get things off their chests to God and thus pass their burdens on to God; they can then praise God for taking the burden from them, for hearing prayer and promising to answer it. That is how the life of prayer is supposed to work. Jeremiah, too, makes this transition from urgent prayer or protest (20:7-10) to a declaration of trust in God (20:11), followed by a specific petition for matters to be put right (20:12), and then by confession of his praise (20:13). Having expressed his inner turmoil, he thus goes on to declare that he has confidence in Yahweh, nevertheless.

> But Yahweh is with me like a fearsome warrior.
> Therefore my persecutors will stumble. They will not prevail.
> They will be bitterly ashamed because they have not

> succeeded.
> Their disgrace will last forever, it will not be forgotten.
> Almighty Yahweh, righteous in his testing,
> the one who sees into heart and mind,
> let me see your vengeance upon them,
> since it was to you that I committed my cause.
> Sing to Yahweh, praise Yahweh!
> He rescues the needy from the power of evil people!
> (20:11-13).

But these words of confidence, expectation, and praise are not the end of what Jeremiah has to say to God. He cannot, in fact, quite hold on to this conviction that God is with him. He has not forgotten those words about trust. But he is torn apart because faith and praise wrestle for possession of his heart with doubt and despair, and he cannot quite endure the strain of this tension.

> Curse the day I was born!
> May the day my mother bore me never be blessed!
> Curse the man who brought the news to my father,
> "It's a boy! You have a son!",
> making him so glad.
> May that man be like the cities
> that Yahweh overthrew without pity,
> may he hear a cry in the morning and an alarm at noon,
> because he did not kill me at birth,
> so that my mother would have become my grave,
> and her womb would have been enlarged for ever.
> Why did I come out of the womb,
> to see trouble and affliction
> and end my life in disgrace? (20:14-18).

Sing to Yahweh, praise Yahweh (verse 13); *curse the day I was born* (verse 14). Who is this man who proclaims that God is judge, *and* that God commits violence and outrage; who declares God's praise, *and* curses the day he was born; who is as hard as a rock outside, but torn apart inside?

What being a prophet costs

The most extraordinary thing is that the chapter ends on that note of despair. Sharing your experiences with other people is relatively easy, when it means acknowledging that you *have been* going through a bad patch, but that the Lord has now brought you out of it. Here is a man who puts into writing where he is spiritually even though that means ending in total darkness. He had no choice and he found no release, because God needed someone to keep warning Judah about the calamity that was coming, and he had to keep living by faith and not by sight over the question whether God was ever going to fulfill the words spoken to and through him.

But why did he write it down? It is rather surprising to find this anti-testimony in a prophetic book. There is nothing quite like it elsewhere in the prophets, though Jeremiah's final cry of despair is paralleled and developed in Job. The other prophets do not tell us much of the intimacy of their relationship with God. Why does Jeremiah do so? Why is there recorded in Scripture the personal and private agonizing of the man of God with God?

One reason may arise out of the fact that it is obviously not easy to be hard as a rock outside when you are being torn apart inside. The tension between the outward proclamation and the inner scream itself threatens to rend the man apart. The scream, indeed, cannot finally be stifled or repressed. It has to receive expression. So writing it down helps to give expression to it in the only way that is possible. It gets it out of the system. That may be one reason why Jeremiah put it in writing.

That is itself striking. But even more remarkable is the fact that Jeremiah's agonizing finds a place in God's book. God, in other words, accepted Jeremiah's complaints and protests and prayers for vengeance on his enemies. God let Jeremiah batter him on the chest, and implicitly encourages us to follow Jeremiah's example. We too may be called to stand hard as a rock. But if we are torn apart inwardly as we have to stand firm outwardly, that inward affliction can receive expression. We need not attempt to bottle it up because God invites us to pour it out. We do not have to deny it; we can acknowledge it to ourselves and to God. We can be honest to God.

Now there is such a thing as effrontery or cheek or impudence, such a thing as failure to treat God as God. The point at which boldness becomes effrontery depends in part on the pressure someone has been put under, on the demands that have been laid upon them. Jeremiah is a person on whom God made total demands. He is a man who comes close to a total commitment. And the man of a unique obedience is entitled to a unique boldness.

I remember once noticing a poster on Nottingham Railway Station: "There is a religion which sees life as a challenge to be met, not as a cross to be born." If there is, then it is not the religion of Jeremiah, nor of Jesus. Nor is it a religion I am very interested in. Because a religion that is worth following has to be able to cope with the fact that life is not always a thrilling challenge; it is sometimes an experience of crucifixion. And being a prophet, or being any kind of faithful servant of God, is not always a thrilling challenge. Sometimes, the experience of the cost, in isolation and opposition, in the loss of any right to run one's own life, in being torn apart even as one is as hard as a rock outside, is rather an experience of crucifixion.

Indeed, arguably, it is at these moments of crucifixion that Christian ministry is at its most authentic, its most distinctive. For that was how it was with Jesus, and that is how it is with the person who follows Jesus.

The parallels between Jeremiah and Jesus are striking. Both experienced isolation and betrayal by those nearest to them. Both experience the loss of family and home and a permanent place to lay their head. Both were inwardly torn apart (in Gethsemane, in Jesus' case) even while they were hard as a rock outside (in the temple or on trial). It is hardly surprising that some people, when asked who they thought Jesus was, suggested he might be Jeremiah reincarnate. Jesus supremely fulfills Jeremiah's kind of calling.

But this does not imply that henceforth God's servants never have to do so. On the contrary, the cost of following Christ is to take up your own cross. When Paul was converted, the Lord described him as "a chosen instrument of mine. For I will show him how much he must suffer for the sake of my name" (Acts 9:15-16).

> ... always being given up to death for Jesus' sake, so that the life of Jesus may be manifested in our mortal flesh (2 Cor. 4:11).

That is how *Christian* ministry works.

There is a cost involved in being a prophet, in being a servant of God. There is a cross involved. We do not have to hide from this fact with glib talk about life being a challenge. Because God promises that as we carry the cross, we can also reveal the glory. Even unknowingly, in his bleakest moments, Jeremiah was doing that. How, will emerge more clearly as we consider who a prophet is identified with.

CHAPTER TWO

Who a prophet is identified with

Why is such a cost involved in being a prophet? How is God's glory revealed in his affliction? In his book on *The Prophets*, the American rabbi Abraham Heschel talks about Jeremiah's sympathy—his sympathy with Israel, and his sympathy with God. Jeremiah feels with, shares the emotions of, Yahweh's people, and Yahweh in person. He is identified with them. It is this identification that costs Jeremiah.

Identification with Israel

Jeremiah was a prophet of doom. He was a man who declared that the collapse of the state was inevitable. How is one to visualize his face as he delivers this message? Would it have an air of triumph and satisfaction? Is Jeremiah the kind of preacher of doom whose message really gives expression to his own hang-ups?

One must grant that Jeremiah had no quarrel with God over whether Jerusalem should be destroyed, and in this sense he would be triumphant and satisfied when it was. But at the same time he was identified with Judah in its affliction. He accepted, but dreaded, its destruction. He prayed for it to be averted. And he accepted a share in its calling and in its suffering.

His anguish finds clear expression in his moving poem concerning a drought that apparently occurred one year in Judah.

> Judah droops, its cities languish,
> its men sink to the ground;
> Jerusalem's cry goes up.
> Their flock-masters send their boys for water,
> they come to the pools but find no water there.
> Back they go, with empty vessels;
> the produce of the land has failed,
> because there is no rain.
> The farmers' hopes are wrecked,
> they uncover their heads for grief.
> The hind calves in the open country and forsakes her young
>   because there is no grass;
> for lack of herbage, wild asses stand on the high bare places
>   and snuff the wind for moisture,
> as wolves do, and their eyes begin to fail (14:2-6 NEB).

So Jeremiah speaks concerning a present calamity. But a prophet is a person of insight, of foresight, of a vivid imagination, someone who experiences things that still belong to the future. Jeremiah goes through all the horror and panic of enemy invasion before it actually occurs.

> I am in anguish! I writhe with pain!
> Walls of my heart!
> My heart is throbbing!
> I cannot keep quiet,
> for I have heard the trumpet call and the cry of war.
> Ruin on ruin is the news
> the whole land is laid waste…

It is as if there has been a nuclear holocaust that leaves nothing on earth but the awful stillness of death.

Who a prophet is identified with

> I looked to the earth, to see a formless waste;
> to the heavens, and their light had gone.
> I looked to the mountains, to see them quaking
> and all the heights astir.
> I looked, to see no man at all,
> the very birds of heaven had fled.
> I looked, to see the wooded country a wilderness,
> all its towns in ruins,
> at the presence of Yahweh,
> at the presence of his burning anger (4:19-20, 23-26 JB).

At the presence of Yahweh! It is God who brings about the calamities of the present and of the imminent future, for they are caused by Judah's turning from God and from God's ways. So Jeremiah's anguish finds expression in his sadness at its spiritual blindness and its false trust.

> How can I bear my sorrow? I am sick at heart,
> Hark, the cry of my people from a distant land:
> 'Is the LORD not in Zion? Is its King no longer there?'
> Why do they provoke me with their images and foreign gods?
> Harvest is past, summer is over, and we are not saved.
> I am wounded at the sight of my people's wound;
> I go like a mourner, overcome with horror.
> Is there no balm in Gilead, no physician there?
> Why has no new skin grown over their wound?
> Would that my head were all water,
> my eyes a fountain of tears,
> that I might weep day and night for my people's dead!
> (8:18-9:1 NEB).

There is a twofold blindness here. First, there is a facile, blithe trust that everything will be all right because God is on our side. "Is the kingly presence of Yahweh not known in Jerusalem, his own royal city?" Yet those who have said, "Don't worry, Yahweh is with us, Yahweh is on our side," have often been mistaken. Then there is, secondly, an inability to recognize that those who seek help from other gods as well as notionally relying on

Yahweh thereby actually forfeit Yahweh's help. No hedging of bets is possible.

So one evidence that the prophet is identified with his people is the anguish that he feels, both at their suffering and at their blindness. There is no cheap preaching of the judgment of God. The authentic declaration of God's judgment on church or nation is delivered with tears in the preacher's eyes. A second expression of the prophet's identification with his people is the fact that he prays for them. Intercession was an integral part of a prophet's calling. A prophet's task was not only to speak on God's behalf to human beings, but also to speak on human beings' behalf to God. Indeed, Jeremiah grants that if he had not prayed for his people, they would have had every reason for resentment against him (18:20). But he had prayed for them. The poem concerning the drought, for instance, continues as a prayer in which Jeremiah leads the people on the occasion of this disaster.

> Though our sins testify against us,
> yet act, O LORD, for thy own name's sake...
> Thou art in our midst, O LORD,
> and thou hast named us thine; do not forsake us...
> Hast thou spurned Judah utterly?
> Dost thou loathe Zion?
> Why hast thou wounded us, and there is no remedy;
> Why let us hope for better days, and we find nothing good,
> for a time of healing, and all is disaster?...
> Can any of the false gods of the nations give rain?
> Or do the heavens send showers of themselves?
> Art thou not God, O LORD, that we may hope in thee?
> It is thou only who doest all these things
>   (14:7,9,19,22 NEB).

Jeremiah prayed, he encouraged them to pray, he prayed on their behalf.

There are actually very few strictly intercessory prayers in the Old Testament. But there are two other kinds of prayers that

Who a prophet is identified with

seem to fulfill a similar function to intercessory prayer and that may be suggestive for our praying. One is the declaration of God's blessing—"May the people prosper, may the king defend the cause of the poor." A number of psalms declare God's blessing in this way (for instance, Ps. 72), and it is an equivalent to what we might call intercession.

The other kind of prayer is when a person identifies with someone else in prayer. Praying on their behalf then means putting oneself in their place, praying as if one was this other person. If I do that, I pray not for "them," but for "me" or "us"—I am so identified with them. It is this that is characteristic of Jeremiah's prayers for his people.

> We acknowledge our wickedness, the wrongdoing of our ancestors. We have sinned against you, Yahweh (14:20).

Jeremiah does not stand aloof from the people in their sin. He identifies with the sinner, as Jesus did in his baptism and on his cross. To intercede for someone involves identifying with them, sharing their situation, standing in their place. Daniel's prayer (Dan. 9) is like this: not "they have sinned, please bring them to repentance," but "we have sinned, please forgive us." At first sight, Moses' prayer for the Israelites' forgiveness is rather different. He acknowledges that the people have committed a gross sin, but pleads for them to be forgiven—otherwise he wishes to die with them (Exod. 32:31,32). Intercession involves standing in someone else's place out of a willingness to identify with the people to whom one has to minister.

We can approach a third aspect to Jeremiah's identification with Israel by asking the question, What do we mean by "Israel"? In an outward sense the answer to that question is clear enough: it is the descendants of the patriarch Israel or Jacob. But in the inward sense, "Israel" means something rather different. Much later, Paul comments that "not all who are descended from Israel belong to Israel" (Rom. 9:6). Indeed, in Paul's day most of the outward Israel did not belong to the inward Israel. Only a small number, a "remnant," recognized Jesus as Messiah and showed that they belonged to the real Israel. Paul himself is the epitome of that small minority (see Rom. 11:1-5).

It was the same in Jeremiah's day; the bulk of Israel had turned their backs on being Israel. On that occasion, too, there was one man who epitomized what it meant to be Israel, Jeremiah himself. Before he was even born, he had been chosen by God, formed by God, known by God, consecrated by God (1:5). He was called to be the one true Israelite, called to stand alone, apart from the crowd, to show the crowd what it should be. His vocation was to incarnate the response to God that all Israel was supposed to make. He had to be willing to be a minority of one.

In the modern western world, people do not mind being distinctive. We enjoy doing our own thing. We would rather stand out from the crowd than be identified with its gray mass (though we may want there to be some in-group with which we do identify). But in most cultures, people have not wanted to be different. Their identity comes in large part from their identification with a community. Jeremiah did not enjoy having to be different. But he had to stand alone—and here is a paradox –precisely because of his identification with Israel. He had to be identified with the Israel of the flesh in his anguish and his prayer. But he also had to be identified with the Israel of the spirit, to be the minority of one, to be the one true Israelite, and in this sense to be a man apart.

Of course it was not God's purpose that responsive Israel should consist of one man and no more. On the contrary, Jeremiah's task was to call all Israel to follow. But only a small number in fact respond. One was Baruch, the scribe who wrote down Jeremiah's prophecies (see Jer. 36). Baruch shared Jeremiah's response to Yahweh and he shared Jeremiah's temptation to despair.

> I give up! The LORD has added sorrow to my troubles. I am worn out from groaning, and I can't find any rest!

We recall Jeremiah's own temptation to give up, to which Yahweh replied that he had to pull himself together, for there was worse to come (11:18-12:6). His reply to Baruch is similar.

> I, the LORD, am tearing down what I have built and pulling up what I have planted. I will do this to the entire earth. Are you looking for special treatment for yourself? Don't do it. I am bringing disaster on all mankind, but you will at least escape with your life, wherever you go. I, the LORD, have spoken (45:3-5 GNB).

"You share Jeremiah's response to me. But this will not gain you exemption from the fate of the nation as a whole. You are identified with the true Israel, and that is great. But you cannot escape being identified also with the fate of the outward Israel. I promise you that your life will be preserved, as Jeremiah's will be. But you have to go through the fall of Jerusalem and the exile. The remnant does not escape the fate of the whole people. It is identified with them."

Yet as Jeremiah and Baruch suffer, their suffering has a different meaning from that of the people as a whole. They do not suffer for their own sins, but for the sins of others. And because they were willing to suffer, others can be blessed and brought nearer to God. Because Jeremiah was willing to suffer, and because Baruch was willing to suffer through being associated with Jeremiah, their lives and their words spoke to their own people. The very existence of Jeremiah's book is an evidence of that. Indeed, if *we* learn from the book of Jeremiah, if it takes us nearer to God and deeper into God, then this is because Jeremiah and Baruch were willing to accept the cost of bringing this book to birth, in being identified both with the true Israel of the promise, and with the outward Israel in its sin and punishment. So we gain through their affliction. But we are also challenged to be ready to accept it ourselves.

It may be that we cannot see ourselves as Jeremiahs. There was something unique about God's dealings with him: he was a prophet. It is more difficult to escape seeing oneself as Baruch. He is the ordinary man who responds to God's word. But his experience hints that there is not, after all, such a difference between what God expects of the "ordinary" believer and how God deals with him, and what God expects of, and how God deals with, the prophet. Jeremiah embodies what it means to be Israel; Baruch embodies the required response to this, of being willing to walk the same way. And this response is the calling of all God's people. What happens to Jeremiah is what happens to the true Israel of God, and if we wish to be associated with the Israel of God then this is what we must accept. Being a prophet involves that identification. But the suffering, the identification, does bear fruit. It contributes to the history of the people of God.

Identification with Yahweh

Jeremiah, we have suggested, is identified with Israel in his anguish, in his praying, and in his suffering. But he is identified also with God, and this further identification manifests itself in similar connections.

Jeremiah is identified with God's anguish, as he is with Israel's. We may return once again to the first of the passages in which Jeremiah wrestles with the cost of being a prophet. Jeremiah's lament (11:18—12:6) is followed by what one can only describe as God's own lament.

> I have forsaken the house of Israel,
> I have cast off my own people.
> I have given my beloved into the power of her foes.
> My people have turned on me like a lion from the scrub,
> roaring against me...
> Many shepherds have ravaged my vineyard
> and trampled down my field,
> they have made my pleasant field a desolate wilderness,
> made it a waste land, waste and waterless, to my sorrow.
> The whole land is waste, and no one cares
> (12:7-8,10-11 NEB).

Here is the anguish of God, shared as part of God's response to Jeremiah's own lament. Jeremiah had asked whether God

Who a prophet is identified with

really cared about how Jeremiah felt and about how Judah was hell-bent on self-destruction. One element in God's response is to ask, "How do you think I feel? Do you think I am a block of stone? Do you think I do not care? Do you think it does not break me, to forsake my house, to surrender my beloved to her enemies?" Jeremiah is invited into the anguish of God.

The same note is sounded in the prayers we referred to above.

> Hope of Israel,
> its savior in time of distress,
> why are you like a stranger in the land,
> like a traveler pitching his tent for a night? (14:8).

Here is a telling description of God, a stranger in God's own country, a homeless vagabond, a tramp.

> Let my eyes stream with tears
> day and night, without ceasing,
> for my maiden daughter, my people,
> is shattered and broken... (14:17).

Here again is Jeremiah sharing the anguish of God. Indeed, it is a puzzle to decide whose anguish is referred to here. Are we reading about God's feelings (as in ch. 12)? Or of Jeremiah's? Von Rad (*Old Testament Theology* Volume 2, p. 193) notes that in Jeremiah the distinction between God's words and the prophet's words becomes obscured. We are not sure whether we are reading lyrical poetry or the word of Yahweh. But the reason why we cannot tell whether we are sharing Jeremiah's anguish or God's is that both are the same thing, because Jeremiah is identified with God. Jeremiah is torn apart not merely because of his own affliction, nor only because of Judah's affliction, but because of the affliction of God, which God allows him to share.

Jeremiah was also identified with Judah in his prayer. At this same point, too, he is called to be identified with God. The record of his prayer is consequently an awesome dialogue between Jeremiah, the voice of Judah, and Jeremiah, the voice of God. He prays on Judah's behalf (14:7-9); but here is God's response:

> These are Yahweh's words to this people: They like their feet to wander, they exercise no control over them. But Yahweh does not accept them. He will now keep their wrong-doing in mind; he will punish their sins (14:10).

In the Old Testament, it was assumed that prayers would be answered. People poured out their sufferings and their longings and their needs before God, and prophet or priest in God's name declared God's response, hopefully the promise of blessing and forgiveness and restoration. But here in Jeremiah it is not that response. *Yahweh does not accept them. He will now keep their wrongdoing in mind.* Indeed, Jeremiah goes on,

> Yahweh said to me, Do not pray for the well-being of this people. When they fast, I will not listen to their cry; when they offer whole-offering and grain-offering, I will not accept them (14:11-12).

A prophet's task is to pray for his people because he is identified with them. But sometimes, because he is also identified with God he has to take "No" for an answer. The point is reasserted in the verses that follow. Jeremiah again prays on his people's behalf, acknowledging their sin, pointing out their needs, testifying to the Lordship of Yahweh, pleading for his mercy (14:19-22). But the response is the same. Indeed, it is perhaps more chilling.

> Yahweh said to me, Even if Moses and Samuel stood before me,
> I would feel nothing for this people (15:1).

Suppose these two great men of prayer, representatives respectively of the Torah and the Prophets, were at this moment to rise from the dead and plead for Judah: their prayers would not be heard.

Here Jeremiah's terrible gift of insight is to see when prayers cannot be answered. Perhaps it is that he can see when prayers are not real and when repentance is not genuine even though the words are quite right. He can see when God's people are past repentance and there is no escape from judgment and no way of averting disaster. And therefore he cannot pray. He cannot ask for the morally impossible. He has to accept identification with God's will. He shares God's longing that prayer should be answered and also God's realization that it cannot be. He shares God's anguish, but God also allows (indeed requires) him to share God's indignation. *I have not kept the company of jokers and enjoyed myself. Because your hand has been upon me, I have lived in isolation, because you have filled me with indignation* (15:17). Jeremiah is distinct from the crowd because he is identified with God's anger as well as with God's anguish. That was why he held himself aloof from the noisy reveling of his contemporaries. It was incompatible with the divine indignation that filled him.

> I am full of the anger of the LORD,
> I cannot hold it in.
> I must pour it out on the children in the street
> and on the young men in their gangs.
> Man and wife alike shall be caught in it,
> the greybeard and the very old.
> Their houses shall be turned over to others,
> their fields and their women alike.
> For I will raise my hand, says the LORD,
> against the people of the country… (6:11-12 NEB).

God feels anguish for the people (and presumably that generates a longing to answer their prayers), but also feels anger toward them (and that means their prayers cannot be answered). The remarkable tension felt by Jeremiah is attributed also to God. Judah is God's people, so God is attached to it. But it is rebellious, so God is determined to punish it. She is God's beloved, and God loves her and grieves over her suffering. But she is an adulteress, and God hates her and has no desire to have her back. We are again reminded of Hosea, who in his own life knew the tension between longing to abandon his wife because she was unfaithful to him and being unable to do so because she was his wife. That is God's position, and Jeremiah's identification with God is an identification with God in the ambiguity of God's relationship with the people.

A final aspect of Jeremiah's identification with God to which we may draw attention is that what people do to him is what they do to God. We may come back to the question of why these accounts of Jeremiah's affliction are in the Bible. Some reasons we have suggested already. Jeremiah wrote them down to give expression to the inner anguish that in his public ministry he had to hide; and Jeremiah (or his followers) believed them to embody what it means to be the people of God, to be the remnant, to be the suffering servant. Yet Jeremiah suffers not merely because he is identified with *Judah*, but also because he is identified with *God*. To be God is to experience rejection and hostility, attack and crucifixion. When people have the opportunity, they crucify God—from the blood of Abel to the blood of Zechariah (Luke 11:51).

So Jeremiah comes to his people as the representative of God, and quite naturally he is crucified. That is perhaps why we are told so many stories about the outward afflictions of Jeremiah in the second half of the book. It is not because someone was interested in writing Jeremiah's biography. It is because what people were doing to Jeremiah they were doing to God and God's word. Jehoiakim dramatically consigns Jeremiah's scroll line by line into the fire—snip... snip... snip (Jer. 36). That is what he did to God's word. And that essentially is what people tried to do to Jeremiah himself over the years. The reason is the fact that Jeremiah is identified with God. He does not talk about what is done to him because *he* is important, but because it reveals something about God. His life and how he is treated exhibits people's attitude to the word. What men do to Jeremiah reflects what they think of God. God himself is the God who suffers, the one who is pushed out of the world onto a cross. God is the crucified one. So in Jeremiah we begin to get a hint of a claim that will be developed in the vision of the suffering servant, that in the affliction of Yahweh's servant the arm of Yahweh is revealed (Isa. 53:1). Jeremiah's life witnesses to this through his identification with God.

CHAPTER THREE

What distinguishes a prophet?

To the modern reader, "the prophets" generally mean well-known great Old Testament figures such as Elijah and Elisha, Amos and Hosea, Isaiah and Micah, Jeremiah and Ezekiel. Our acceptance of the Hebrew Scriptures decides for us who are *the* prophets.

For people living in the time of these prophets, however, matters were more complicated. They were not, in fact, the only "prophets"; the Old Testament refers to many others, though without telling us much about them. Sometimes their names and their words have not survived because they did not have the deep significance that was found in the stories and the messages of *the* prophets. They were honorable, worthy men and women, used by God, but ultimately belonging to that vast army of the faithful whose names are known to God but not to historians. Others of them, however, were people who were quite opposed to the work of prophets such as Jeremiah. They brought a different message. The issues raised by this phenomenon have a prominent place in the book of Jeremiah; distinguishing an authentic prophet from a counterfeit prophet was an important issue in the period in which he lived.

Jeremiah and Hananiah

A story relating to the last years of the independent life of Judah illustrates the questions that were being raised.

The nation of Israel had never been a major power in the world it belonged to, except for a short period in the time of David and Solomon. Usually it was under the authority of one of the bigger nations that commanded empires in the Middle East—Egypt or Assyria before the exile, in subsequent centuries Persia or Greece (or Rome or Byzantium, or Britain or America...). During the time of Jeremiah, power in Mesopotamia passed from the Assyrians to the Babylonians. The time of transition was naturally a time of upheaval. The Babylonians more than once had to suppress attempts to throw off their authority at the edges of their empire. After one such attempt on the part of Judah, in 597 the Babylonians removed King Jehoiachin (Jeconiah) from the throne, and took him to Babylonia, along with many of the other Judean leaders and some of the temple vessels. They replaced Jehoiachin as king by their own nominee, Jehoiachin's uncle Zedekiah. But Zedekiah was a feeble leader, easily pushed this way or that. He was soon under pressure from within Judah and from the other vassal states in the area (Edom, Moab, Ammon, and so on) to rebel against the Babylonians once again.

At this time, Jeremiah sent messages to Zedekiah to the effect that there ought to be no rebellion against Babylon. It is Yahweh who has given power over the area to Nebuchadrezzar, the Babylonian king. His authority ought to be accepted until Yahweh takes it away from him again. The Judeans, in particular, are not to listen to voices declaring that the vessels of Yahweh's house, the temple of Solomon, would soon be returned. On the contrary, if Judah does not submit it will lose the rest of the treasured vessels and fittings of the temple, and indeed will lose its very land itself as the people are taken off to join Jehoiachin in exile (Jer. 27).

What distinguishes a prophet?

Jeremiah's words were in direct conflict, however, with those of another prophet, Hananiah, who declared that Yahweh would indeed soon bring the temple vessels back to Jerusalem. The Babylonian yoke would be broken (Jer. 28:1-11).

So who is the authentic prophet? How are people to decide? What are the marks of a true prophet that differentiate him from a false prophet? As we look back on the story of Jeremiah at the time of this confrontation with Hananiah, it is easy to know whose side we are on. It is quite clear who is the good guy, who the bad guy. History has passed its verdict. But that was not the case for people living at the time.

There is often a similar difficulty about evaluating the alleged prophets of our own age. There are many "prophetic" figures in the world today—those who declare that the world, or particular societies, or particular institutions are on the wrong track and must radically reconsider what they are doing. There are the conservation movement, the anti-psychiatry movement (R. D. Laing, Thomas Szasz), and the anti-education movement (Ivan Illich). There are many "prophetic" movements within the church, such as liberation theology and various voices in the World Council of Churches. Nearer home for many people, there are those who claim "the gift of prophecy" or similar gifts and proclaim in congregational worship that "this is the word of the Lord." How do we tell which are the words of the Lord?

There were apparently no outward differences between Jeremiah and Hananiah. Both exercised a public ministry in the temple before the priests and people. Both prophesied in the name of Yahweh, "Thus says Almighty Yahweh, the God of Israel." Both stood in respectable Israelite traditions. Jeremiah might remind one of Hosea, as we have seen, or of Micah (in ch. 26 it is the similarity of Jeremiah's gloomy message to Micah's that leads to his escaping being lynched for speaking of God bringing disaster on Jerusalem). But Hananiah in turn might remind one of Deuteronomy (which promised that a people that reformed itself, as in some ways Judah had in the time of Josiah, would be blessed by God) and of Isaiah (who had promised Jerusalem's deliverance in his day in terms quite similar to those used by Hananiah).

Both Jeremiah and Hananiah used "symbolic actions." Jeremiah made his preaching concrete by putting on the ox-yoke (the ball and chain, as it were) that Judah was destined for. Hananiah made his preaching concrete by breaking these. There was apparently no difference between Jeremiah and other prophets in the unusual behavior they exhibited when they were (allegedly) in touch with God. Jeremiah 29 speaks of the high priest having authority over every madman who prophesies—and the category includes Jeremiah (29:26-7). Now Jeremiah does not speak of the "spirit" coming on him (a phrase that suggests a special experience of the power and presence of God that often made someone act in abnormal ways) as earlier and later prophets do (e.g., 2 Kings 2; Ezek. 11). But apparently his contemporaries did not notice a difference here. One may note a Christian parallel in the use of tongues and other gifts outside the Christian community, or within it but for the glory of lords other than Jesus (1 Cor. 12:2-3). There is no outward difference in the exercise of the gift.

There is no apparent difference in the means by which the prophet claims to receive his message. Jeremiah has visions (e.g., Jer. 1; 4:19-31), and so do the other prophets (23:16). Jeremiah has dreams (31:26); so do the other prophets (23:27-8).

Perhaps, then, being in truth entrusted with God's word gives a prophet a special boldness or conviction, so that this prophet's manner or bearing is somehow different from those of the person who has no real commission from God? Apparently not. When Hananiah broke the symbolic ox-yoke from Jeremiah's neck and declared that Yahweh was about to break the Babylonian yoke from the nation's neck in the same way (Jer. 28: 10-11), it is Hananiah who seems to have the real authority. He has the last word. Jeremiah the prophet *goes his way*: tail between his legs, defeated again. We are once more reminded of the Paul of 2 Corinthians, derided as a someone who could be all things to all people when it suited him, good at writing letters

What distinguishes a prophet?

but poor at face-to-face confrontation, unimpressive in the cut-and-thrust of argument (2 Cor. 10:10), rather feeble compared with the real apostles the Corinthians are enthralled by.

Now in the end, though Hananiah won this battle of words (and of symbolic actions), it was a costly victory. The chilling final verses of the story (Jer. 28:12-17) relate how Jeremiah declares sentence of death on Hananiah for *uttering rebellion against Yahweh*, and within two months Hananiah is dead. But at the time of the confrontation, one might have been hard pressed to decide whether Hananiah or Jeremiah was nearer to the mind of Yahweh. So what does distinguish an authentic prophet?

"Concerning the Prophets"

Clearly this question will have been of huge importance to Jeremiah. His own attempts to identify what was wrong with the other prophets are collected most systematically in a section of his book headed, *"Concerning the prophets"* (Jer. 23:9-40).

His analysis opens with a spirited lament at what might be called their moral and theological relativism: they fail to maintain God's standards with regard to ethics and with regard to faith. Jeremiah begins by describing one of those moments of anguish and indignation I referred to earlier. Yahweh has spoken holy words and they have a devastating effect on Jeremiah himself. *My heart is broken within me, all my bones shake* (23:9 RSV). Probably both those phrases are misleading in English. The "heart" in Hebrew thinking refers to the seat of intelligence and decision-making. Later, Jeremiah speaks of the false prophets' *visions of their own minds* and of the intentions of God's *mind* (23:16,20), and in both places it is the Hebrew word for "heart" that is used. At the beginning of his lament, then, he is not referring to the breaking of his heart (in our sense) but to the blowing of his mind. And his bones shaking is another way of expressing the same thing—I was shattered, we might say. God has brought home to him the enormity of what is going on in Judah. The calamities they experience have come upon them because of the immorality and injustice that abound: *the land is full of adulterers.... Their speed is in doing evil and their strength is in doing what is not right* (23:10). Furthermore, prophet and priest are just as involved as anyone, and their wrongdoing takes place even in the temple itself (23:11). They follow the people in their sin instead of leading them from it. This is the first element in Jeremiah's indictment of the other prophets.

The second element in their moral and theological relativism links with this. They encourage adultery and deceit rather than turning people from it. The prophets of the northern kingdom in the old days were bad enough. They led Israel astray, encouraging it to worship the Canaanite Baals (23:13). Their theology was manifestly unorthodox. But there is a sense in which the theology Jeremiah finds among his fellow prophets in Jerusalem is even more twisted. They prophesy in the name of Yahweh, the holy God, and in Yahweh's name they encourage evil. What Jeremiah sees is not merely *unsavory* (23:13) *but repulsive* (23:14).

The prophets of Jerusalem are failing, in fact, at a point at which the Torah warns that prophets may fail. Deuteronomy twice discusses the significance of prophecy and the problem of distinguishing true from false prophecy. The succession of prophets would be God's way of providing the guidance his people needed, which in Moses' day they received from Moses himself (18:15-19). But a prophet who leads Israel after other gods, encouraging "wickedness" and "rebellion" against Yahweh, is to be put to death (13:1-11). Thus Jeremiah declares that the prophets *strengthen the hands of evildoers, so that no-one turns from their wickedness;* and therefore they will forfeit their lives (Jer. 23:14-15). He declares judgment on Hananiah because he has encouraged *rebellion* (28:16: the same rare Hebrew word is used here and in Deut. 13:5—and also in Jer. 29:32).

So Jeremiah claims that by their attitude the prophets cut themselves off from the company of those who take the Torah

What distinguishes a prophet?

seriously. They are working against it.

Further, the other prophets preach empty hope instead of unpleasant truth. They are continually saying, "*All will go well with you*" *to people who despise Yahweh's word. They say to all who follow the inclinations of their own stubbornness, "No trouble will come upon you"* (23:16,17). They say, "It will be well with you"—*shalom* to you. As Jeremiah has put it earlier, they have treated my people's wound superficially, saying *"All will be well, all will be well"—when it will not* (6:14;8:11). There is no *shalom*; but they say, *shalom, shalom*. In order to emphasize the quality of something in Hebrew, often the word itself will be repeated. The Song of Songs is the best song; holy, holy, holy (repeating the word three times) suggests *ultimate* holiness. Thus shalom, shalom is perfect peace. "Thou dost keep him in perfect peace, whose mind is stayed on thee," Isaiah says (26:3 RSV): thou dost keep him in *shalom shalom*. But in the time of Jeremiah *shalom shalom* is the promise of the false prophets. The characteristic word of the true prophet, Jeremiah claims, is that there is trouble to come. Jeremiah reminds Hananiah that their predecessors had generally spoken of *war, famine, and plague* (28:8). So Hananiah and the other prophets of Jeremiah's day stand outside the authentic prophetic tradition, as well as beyond the Torah.

Now of course the prophet's motive in warning of disaster was a positive one. His aim was to bring people to repentance. He was trying to be constructive. The other prophets look as if they are being constructive. They appear to be trying to build up the people's faith, hope and confidence. But Ezekiel, in his discussion of false prophecy (Ezek. 13), offers two vivid descriptions of them. They look as if they are strengthening Israel, but actually they are only whitewashing a wall (papering over the cracks, we would say); and wallpaper and whitewash will not stop it collapsing. Or they are like foxes scavenging among ruins, instead of people who have seriously gone up into the breaches or built up a wall for the house of Israel. When the day of Yahweh's anger comes, the wall will collapse. Their constructive-*looking* ministry is destructive in *effect*. What is needed is to bring Israel to its senses. That is why the characteristic word of a true prophet speaks of calamity.

The characteristic word, that is. Jeremiah does speak of hope for the future. He promises that a branch will grow from the tree of David that is being cut down, a righteous branch, and a new exodus will take the people out of the bondage that is coming, and will eclipse the memory of the first exodus (23:5-8). He promises a restoration of the joy that is being taken away and the establishing of a better relationship between God and his people than they enjoyed under the old covenant. He promises *shalom*, in fact (29:11;33:6). But it is to be peace after conflict, restoration after disaster; no peace without chastisement and repentance.

There, then, are three characteristics of false prophecy; their opposites will characterize true prophecy. If the false prophets followed the people in their sin instead of leading them from it, then a true prophet will be one whose own life is an embodiment of God's truth. A true prophet will be someone who is capable of standing out from the vices of contemporaries, even of the rest of God's people. If someone brings "prophetic" words, but the person's own life is no better than average, we may be suspicious of the prophecy. As was the case with Jeremiah, a prophet's life is part of the message.

Then, if the false prophets encouraged adultery and deceit instead of resisting it, an authentic prophet will be one who brings home God's moral demands. This prophet will be one who perceives where people are ignoring God's standards and where they despise God's word. For God's people delude themselves just as unbelievers do. They become blind to aspects of God's teaching, fool themselves that they are living committed lives, and produce sophisticated rationalizations for sin. Often the next generation can see it, but part of the blindness is that one cannot see it in oneself. Here is where the people of God always need prophets, who will enable us to break through the blindness and deafness of our particular

What distinguishes a prophet?

cultural relativity.

Again, if the false prophets offered vain hopes instead of unpleasant truth, then a true prophet is one who dares say what goes against the grain, what will not be welcome. Contemporary "charismatic" prophecy tends to be encouraging and reassuring. But in Jeremiah's day the promise of God's presence and God's love was the message of the false prophets.

Admittedly doom is not always God's word through prophets. Much of the books of Isaiah and Ezekiel, and (as we have noted) some of Jeremiah's own words, concerned hope for the future. But even here words of comfort and consolation are tied up in different ways with words about calamity; there is no papering over cracks. Furthermore, in each situation a prophet is confronting the attitudes of the people being addressed. Even the message of peace is one that confronts, rather than colludes with, the attitudes of those the prophet has to speak to. Isaiah refers to the possibility of trusting in the power and the promises of Yahweh but speaks to people who do not want to believe in these and are inclined to rely on political stratagems. Ezekiel and Isaiah 40–55 speak of restoration for the exiles, but speak to people who do not wish to be lifted from the morass of depression and doubt into which the reality of God's judgment has taken them. Haggai and Zechariah declare that the temple will be rebuilt, but address people who no longer believe that Yahweh will fulfill the promises about that and have abandoned attempts to live as if Yahweh will do so. Whether it is words about disaster or words of hope, prophecy is confrontational and is addressed to the specific circumstances in which the prophet ministers. So the real prophet is the one who is prepared to confront and who is able to tell whether this is a day of calamity or a day of hope.

In these ways, then, authentic prophecy resists moral and theological relativism. The other major feature of Jeremiah's critique of the prophets is that their words have no origin outside themselves. The point is made negatively by describing where their messages did not come from. They have not *stood in*

Yahweh's council to see and hear his word (23:18). Yahweh's council is the heavenly equivalent to the city council or the parish council or the county council. It is the place where decisions are made about policy, strategy and action in heaven and on earth. The Old Testament includes several vivid descriptions of it: Yahweh and the sons of God discussing the spirituality of Job (Job 1–2); Yahweh and the host of heaven determining judgment on Ahab (1 Kings 22); God holding judgment on the "gods" themselves in the divine council (Ps. 82); Yahweh commissioning agents to begin the process of comforting the people, these agents declaring that Yahweh's way home to Jerusalem is to be prepared, a voice commissioning the prophet to preach to the exiles despite the despair the prophet shares with them (Isa. 40). The privilege of a prophet is to be allowed to listen to the debate in this heavenly council. But *who has stood in Yahweh's council to see and hear his word? Who has paid attention to my word and heard it?* (23:18). The only person of whom that can be true is the person who declares a message about calamity, the one who speaks of storm and wrath, of tempest and anger (23:19-20). Those are the plans that are being formulated in heaven.

How does Jeremiah know? He knows in his own heart, ultimately, only because he believes he *has* stood in Yahweh's council. That is just part of his experience. He cannot prove that it was real; experience cannot be validated like that. He can describe it but he cannot prove its authenticity. People in general can talk about their deepest spiritual experiences, but we cannot thereby prove the validity of what we testify to. The experiences have to be real to us; Jeremiah's experience is truly the foundation of his ministry. But he cannot communicate the nature of his experience in such a way as to prove its authenticity.

So how were people to know that Jeremiah's message was true? One test, though it is little help when the prophecy is delivered, is the test of time. *Yahweh's anger will not turn aside until he has completely accomplished the intentions of his mind. In time you will understand this clearly* (23:20). History will prove Jeremiah right.

What distinguishes a prophet?

Like Isaiah (see Isa. 8:16), Jeremiah wrote down his prophecies so that they could be checked against events in due course. They will be there on record when the moment of truth comes.

Jeremiah's prophecies came to be put together after his ministry was over and he had been proved right over the fall of Jerusalem. This seems to have been a period when there was a crisis over prophecy. So much prophecy had been discredited by the collapse of the state. We need to keep recalling that, although with hindsight we know this was only false prophecy, at the time it was just "prophecy." Authentic and false prophecy were difficult to distinguish. So it was prophecy itself that was in danger of being discredited. Furthermore, there was thus a danger that the real word of Yahweh would be ignored. At this point, in the exile, the test of fulfillment was very important. Certainly most prophecy had been discredited. But the person who is genuinely seeking God's word will not let the true be lost with the false.

The church in subsequent centuries has several times had to deal with excess and falsehood proclaimed in the name of the spirit of prophecy. This happened in Corinth; it happened with the Montanists. In the latter case, the catholic church stifled Montanism and drove it out of the church. Paul's own approach, however, was to deal firmly with excess, but to strive not to quench the Spirit. Long before, Jewish leaders in the exile were doing the same: they acknowledged that prophecy had gone wrong, but urged attention to that prophecy that had been in truth Yahweh's word and had now been vindicated by events. That they succeeded is evidenced by the fact that the author of Isaiah 40–55 can appeal to the fulfilled prophecies of before the exile (*earlier things have clearly come about*) and build on them by *declaring fresh things* (42:9). Second Isaiah's promises are very like those of the false prophets that Jeremiah condemns, but they are distinct from them because they begin by affirming that judgment had indeed been God's word at that point. There is a certain value, then, in seeking to distinguish true from false by whether it comes true.

So Jeremiah's first distinguishing mark that characterizes what is true over against what is false is the mark of religious experience: the true prophet has stood in Yahweh's council. But that cannot be seen. The second is that a prophet's words find fulfillment. But that cannot be seen until it happens. The third mark takes us back to the point made earlier in this collection of material on prophecy. *I did not send the prophets; it was they who ran. I did not speak to them; it was they who prophesied. If they had stood in my council, they would have proclaimed my words to my people. They would have turned them from the utterly evil course on which they are engaged* (23:21-22). The visible mark of prophecy is, do the prophets turn people away from their evil way? Do they follow them in sin or lead them from it? Do they encourage adultery and deceit or resist it? Do they offer vain hope or unpleasant truth? The person who has stood in Yahweh's council meets the moral test, because this prophet has been privy to the formulating of a moral policy.

The message of other prophets did not come from having stood in Yahweh's council. It came, to put the point positively, simply from themselves (23:23-32). Ask these prophets where they get their messages. They relate their dreams, for instance (23:25). Now in principle dreams are a means of revelation that God can use. Joel promises a time when all sorts of people will dream dreams and see visions (Joel 2:28-29). But in these examples in Jeremiah's time, anyway, there is a world of difference between a human being's dream and Yahweh's word. *So let the prophet who has a dream relate this dream, but let the one who has my word speak my word in truth* (23:28). Let us grant that dreams can be a means of the Lord's message coming. Today we see even more clearly than people may have seen in Jeremiah's day that dreams are usually the means whereby our own subconscious finds expression. There is a world of difference between a human being's dream and the Lord's word—the difference between straw and wheat; for Yahweh's word is like fire, or like a hammer that can shatter rock (23:28,29).

The false prophets' messages come from their own mind.

What distinguishes a prophet?

Jeremiah declares that as they *prophesy lies,* they *prophesy the deceptions of their own mind* (23:26); they *prophesy lies in my name* (23:25). To speak or act in God's name is to speak or act as God, as if you were God in person. It is to claim to be God's mouthpiece. The Jews came later to be so wary of a mistake when they took God's name on their lips that they avoided uttering God's name at all. At least they thereby recognized how solemn it is to speak of God. Jeremiah hears his contemporaries flaunting Yahweh's name but attaching it to their own thoughts.

Further, they derive their messages from each other (23:30). I once went to a parish church and heard a brilliant sermon on the promise that "one who believes shall not make haste" (Isa. 28:16). A few weeks later, I found the sermon word for word in a book by J. A. T. Robinson. Why should a man preach someone else's sermon? Because he was under pressure and did not have time to prepare one? This might be defensible, though arguably he ought to attribute it! Or was it because he had nothing to say? Presumably that was the case with the false prophets. They were not in touch with God; they were not privy to his council. But they had to say something. So they borrowed each other's sermons.

Again, the other prophets' words came from their own mouths: they *have only to move their tongues to utter oracles* (23:31 JB). They have the gift of the gab. They will never be lost for words. That is a great gift. But one needs to recall that fluency does not prove that one is in touch with God. It means that if we do not receive words, we will be able to make them up. Jeremiah was aware from the beginning of not having this gift. *Lord Yahweh, I do not know how to speak* (1:6). When Hananiah contradicted him, Jeremiah had no answer. But at least it meant that when he did speak it was because he had Yahweh's words; he was not merely exercising his own big mouth.

The false prophets' messages came not from Yahweh's council, but from their own dreams, from their own minds, from each other, from their own mouths. Jeremiah's material *"Concerning the prophets"* closes on a different note. *When this people, or a prophet or priest, ask you, "What is the burden of Yahweh's message?" you are to say to them, "You are the burden, and I am going to get rid of you"* (23:33; the following verses develop the point). There was something profoundly wrong with the prophets. But there was also something profoundly wrong with their audience, and a congregation gets the prophets it deserves. You are Yahweh's burden, says Jeremiah, with your frivolous attitude to God's word to you. So while we ought to be critical in our approach to prophecy, we also must be self-critical over our own attitude to the word of God.

What makes a false prophet?

Questions concerning the nature of true and false prophecy have aroused considerable interest in Old Testament study in recent years. In one of the books on this subject, *Prophetic Conflict: Its Effect upon Israelite Religion*, James L. Crenshaw includes an analysis of why false prophecy was inevitable. "Inevitable" is a discouraging word; it ought not to excuse us from a determination to resist the pressures that in Israel led to false prophecy. If we are willing to learn from history, we may be able to avoid repeating its mistakes.

One factor that influences a prophet to speak false rather than true is a desire for acceptance. A prophet wants to be right, but also wants to be listened to, and may sincerely want both of these for God's sake. But both may not be possible; in Israel, indeed, they were regularly mutually exclusive. It is clear in Jeremiah's case (and even clearer in Isaiah 40–55) that God's servant contributes to God's purpose by accepting failure and opposition. The desire to succeed, even to gain a hearing for God, can be the desire of the false prophet.

A second threat to authentic prophecy is the institution. In Israel this meant the monarchy. Now the great age of prophecy is the period of the monarchy. The first great prophet is Samuel, in the time of Saul, and the last prophets whose ministry we can explicitly date, Haggai and Zechariah, offer the Old Testament's last account of a Davidic prince's activity in Israel. In part, it was

What distinguishes a prophet?

the monarchy that called forth prophecy. But prophecy's function in relation to the monarchy was to stand up to its attempts to absolutize its own position. Naturally, this stand would lead to attempts on the monarchy's part to stifle prophecy (as the story of Jeremiah illustrates). So the relationship between prophecy and the monarchy is paradoxical and ambivalent, and one of the temptations that come to prophets will be the subordinating of their prophecy to the power of the monarchy. Another embodiment of the institution in Israel is the temple and its priesthood, and there is characteristically a further tension between organized religion and prophecy. The official pressure on Jeremiah to moderate his message (and thus to abandon authentic prophecy) comes from Pashhur in the temple as well as Jehoiakim in the palace.

The pressure of the temple leads us to a fourth threat to authentic prophecy, the power of popular religion. Sometimes this may be overtly syncretistic religion, such as the baalism Jeremiah opposes but of which he accuses other prophets. On other occasions it may be a faith that is Yahwistic in its outward expression. Hananiah prophesied in the name of Yahweh and picked up the emphases of popular religion: "God is on our side, we shall overcome." Popular religion is perhaps most often characterized by an easy optimism of this kind. But the exile marks the transition to another kind of popular religion, a widespread conviction that Yahweh has abandoned his people. It is this conviction that the later message of Ezekiel and that of Isaiah 40-55 has to combat. Here, too, prophets may well be tempted to accede to popular conviction, which could sound very pious. But if they do so, they are inauthentic prophets because they have missed the transition from the day of disaster to the day of grace. The prophet has to be wary of both the optimism and the pessimism of popular religion.

Popular (Yahwistic) religion can take as its ally Yahwistic religious tradition. As we noted above, Hananiah's assurance that Yahweh would look after the fortunes of Judah was based on authentic streams of Israelite belief, the Psalms' commitment to David and to Zion that was emphasized also by Isaiah, and the promises of Deuteronomy that a nation that reformed itself would find a life of blessing. The trouble with Hananiah was only that his message belonged to the previous century. He let himself be led astray because he found something in what was authentic tradition, in the past words of God, but it led him into inauthentic prophecy.

Crenshaw's final reason for the development of false prophecy was the increasing stress on the individual that characterized the period of the exile. This raised more sharply the question of whether God treats individuals with justice, and leads to the temptation to try to justify the ways of God with humanity, and perhaps encouraged some prophets to promise peace because trouble would be unfair to those within the nation who were faithful to God.

The pressures upon a prophet are such that it may not only be inevitable that there are false prophets. It may also be unavoidable that a prophet whose is fundamentally committed to the truth nevertheless sometimes falls into error. Certainly Jeremiah does so. But we shall see in the next chapter that this is not the end of the road for him.

CHAPTER FOUR

What makes someone a prophet?

So being a prophet requires a willingness to accept the cost of serving God in this way. It means accepting the tension of a twofold identification, with God's anguish and indignation, and with Israel's anguish and high calling. It means standing boldly in confrontation with human beings without ever being quite able to prove that the words that you declare are ones that you have overheard in Yahweh's council. So what keeps Jeremiah to this task? How is it that he can find no escape from it?

Jeremiah's Call

Several of the prophets tell us how they came to receive their prophetic calling. In the cases of Isaiah and Amos, the account comes in the midst of their books, but in each case at a significant point. Isaiah's (Isa. 6) marks the beginning of the story of the prophet's confrontation with King Ahaz, a battle to get king and people to take their God seriously in their political life. It is a battle Isaiah will lose, a time when he will look defeated. But he prefaces the story with the account of his call, as if to say, "This is why my word is going to come true even though Ahaz ignores it, because my word has its origin in an occasion when I myself was confronted by God, the holy one of Israel, enthroned in heaven and worshipped by the host of heaven."

It is the same with Amos (Amos 7). King Jeroboam's representative advises Amos that he would be wise to publish his declarations of judgment on Jeroboam in a less indiscreet location than Jeroboam's personal royal chapel at Bethel. "Whose idea do you think it was that I came here?" asks Amos. "Do you think I enjoy risking my life? I did not choose to be a prophet. I was not brought up in the manse. The Lord took me, the Lord sent me."

When Jeremiah and Ezekiel tell us at the beginning of their books how they became prophets, their accounts also provide the background and the justification for the prophecies that follow. We may imagine Jeremiah standing on the temple mount or in the Damascus Gate at Jerusalem, where people gathered for trade and gossip and judicial proceedings. "This is Yahweh's word" he says. Listen for the responses of the shopkeepers in the gate: "O, come on Jeremiah, why should we believe you?" Watch the priests in their huddles: "This man is anti-Israelite, he is dangerous, he will have to be dealt with." As he hears those responses to his preaching, it is the account of how Yahweh commissioned him to be a prophet that comes back to Jeremiah. He is supported in and kept to his prophetic task because in the thirteenth year of the reign of Josiah the son of Amon, king of Judah (626 BC), Yahweh spoke to him.

> Yahweh's word came to me:
>> Before I formed you in the womb, I acknowledged you;
>> before you were born, I set you apart;
>> I appointed you as a prophet to the nations.
>
> I said,
>> But sovereign Yahweh, I do not know how to speak.
>> I am only a young man.
>
> But Yahweh said to me,
>> Do not say, "I am only a young man,"

What makes someone a prophet?

> because you are to go to anyone to whom I send you,
> and to say anything that I tell you.
> Do not be afraid of them,
> because I will be with you to keep you safe.
> This is Yahweh's message.
>
> Then Yahweh put out his hand, touched my mouth, and said to me,
>
> I have put my words in your mouth.
> Today I have appointed you over nations and kingdoms,
> to uproot and to demolish,
> to destroy and to overthrow,
> to build and to plant (1:4-10).

Four moments or aspects of Jeremiah's calling as a prophet may perhaps be distinguished here. Jeremiah begins by recalling, "Yahweh chose me." As Yahweh actually put it, *I acknowledged you*. Jeremiah uses the ordinary verb for "to know," which generally means the same in Hebrew as it does in English—I know my wife, I know the date, I know the English language. But sometimes in the Old Testament (especially in the prophets), it means something more. Jeremiah himself speaks of people not knowing God's standards of conduct (5:4-5), and he means not merely that they were not acquainted with the Torah, but that they did not acknowledge the Torah. To know is to acknowledge, to recognize, to commit oneself to. It involves the will as well as the understanding. Again, in Amos God says to Israel, "You only have I known of all the families of the earth" (Amos 3:2). Not that God was unaware of the existence of the other nations, but he was uniquely committed to Israel.

So it was between God and Jeremiah. God knew Jeremiah before he was born. God took notice of him. God thought about him. God owned him. *Before I formed you in the womb*. Jeremiah no doubt knew quite well where babies came from. But here he ignores the human agency involved in reproduction, like the psalmist who recalls that God knit us together in our mother's womb (Ps. 139:13). The same agent who was responsible for Jeremiah existing at all was responsible for his call to God's service. "*I formed you in the womb*—but before even that, *I* knew you. I acknowledged you, I committed myself to you." The God who was destining him for a certain sphere of service was Lord of every experience that came to him even before his call, even when he was in the womb. *Before you were born I set you apart*, designated you for a specific, particular role. Jeremiah's words were picked up by Paul and used to describe his call: God set him apart before he was born (Gal. 1:15).

In particular, God says, *I appointed you as a prophet to the nations.* The words that Yahweh was to give him were ones that referred not merely to individuals and their private lives, not even merely to the whole people of God. They involved the international powers. If Jeremiah was to bring any serious message to Judah in his day, it had to involve politics and international affairs. Individualistic piety was not enough; God's concerns were wider than that. So the man with God's message finds himself saying things that involve the nations. It can be dangerous enough (or at least potentially humiliating) to confront the people of God with what you claim is God's message. To speak of political and national affairs can be even more uncomfortable. But Jeremiah can look back on Yahweh's saying, *I appointed you as a prophet to the nations.*

So here is a man who has not yet been born. But God has paid attention to Jeremiah, made a commitment to him, set him apart for a particular task, and given him a role with an international significance in the total divine purpose. *I acknowledged you.... I set you apart.... I appointed you....* This is where Jeremiah would begin when asked, "Why should we believe you?" The answer is, "Yahweh chose me."

Then, he would go on, "Yahweh called me." Choice becomes the call when God puts the choice into words to the person in mind, and it is this experience that Jeremiah recalls in the opening chapter of his book. There was a specific moment to which Jeremiah could look back, when he heard God's voice telling him what his place in God's purpose was.

The Bible and Christian history are full of stories of how

What makes someone a prophet?

particular individuals were called to particular roles in God's service. The experiences have a concreteness about them that makes them different from anything that happens to many people today, and we wonder whether the experience was real. Indeed, perhaps the shopkeepers in the gate responded rather skeptically to Jeremiah. "Come on, Jeremiah, how do you know you are not fooling yourself? Lots of unbalanced people think they have been called by God." Perhaps Jeremiah anticipated that objection, because something he tells us about his call and about his reaction to Yahweh's words to him speaks to this hypothetical question. *I said, "But sovereign Yahweh, I do not know how to speak. I am only a young man."* How old Jeremiah actually was we do not know, but the reaction tells us how old (or rather how young) he felt. "Lord, I'm not experienced enough, I'm not wise enough, I haven't had the training. I read the message of Isaiah or Micah, I listen to the confident sermons of contemporary prophets, and I feel I can't compete with that."

This was Jeremiah's reaction to God's call. So later, when questioned or challenged, he can look back on it and say, "I did not want to be a prophet. Indeed even now I often wish I were not. I tried to get out of the task. But Yahweh overcame my unwillingness. Yahweh called me."

Yahweh's response to Jeremiah's hesitation is to remind him that he will give Jeremiah the words to speak. *Do not say, "I am only a young man, because you are to go to anyone to whom I send you, and to say anything that I tell you* (1:7). The theme is continued subsequently: *Yahweh put out his hand, touched my mouth, and said to me, "I have put my words in your mouth"* (1:9). At the beginning of his ministry God gives Jeremiah a message that he is to deliver throughout the years that follow. But also throughout that ministry God will continue giving him his words: *you are to say anything that I tell you.*

It would indeed be a demanding calling to have the right words for all those situations and people that Jeremiah had to address: the right words for people whose eyes seemed to be shut to God's truth, eyes he longed to be a means of Yahweh's opening so that they could see the truth and respond to it; the right words for people like Baruch who did respond, words of encouragement or challenge, of reassurance or rebuke; the right words for the authorities with which he had to deal. How could a man have the right words in all these circumstances? *Sovereign Yahweh, I do not know how to speak.... You are to say anything that I tell you.... I have put my words in your mouth.*

There is one further element in Jeremiah's recollection of his call to which we should draw attention. Consider again those priests in the temple court plotting to dispose of Jeremiah. Here, too, the account of his call has something to say. "Yahweh protects me." *Do not be afraid of them, because I will be with you to keep you safe. This is Yahweh's message* (1:8). There is a clear logical sequence about God's words here. First, *I will be with you*. Here is one of the Bible's recurrent promises. "Yahweh of hosts is with us" (Ps. 46:7, 11). "His name shall be called Emmanuel—which means, God with us" (Matt. 1:23). "Lo, I am with you always" (Matt. 28:20). I will be with you. Therefore, secondly, *I will keep you safe*. Whether it is from the hordes of foreign armies (as in Psalm 46), or from the power of sin (as in Matthew 1), or from the forces that oppose the gospel (as in Matthew 28), you will be delivered. Therefore, thirdly, *do not be afraid*. The sequence is completely logical. "Yahweh protects me." But I suspect Jeremiah must have puzzled over those promises a few times. "God is with me. God delivers me. I need not be afraid. That is what the promise says. So I get put in the stocks, lowered into a cistern, imprisoned in the court of the guard, and finally carted off into obscurity in Egypt. God is with me?" It sounds like the beginning to one of those Jewish jokes that are so profound in their acceptance of the trouble that it has meant to be a Jew: "Lord, if this is what it means to have you with me, what is it like to have you *against* me?"

Yet somehow, it is true that Yahweh is with Jeremiah to keep him safe. Jeremiah is the suffering prophet, the weeping prophet, the life and soul of the funeral. But that is a road he walks with God. *I will be with you, to keep you safe. So do not be afraid of them*. The King James Version has, "be not afraid of their faces." It may be an over-translation, but nevertheless it's very true to Jeremiah. All the indications suggest that Jeremiah was not by nature a bombastic, confident extrovert. He did not enjoy being a prophet; he tried to get out of it more than once. He did not like having to confront people. It was not his nature. All the more significant, then, is Yahweh's encouragement. Do not be afraid of their faces, or of their presence, or of having to confront them. Because I will be with you to keep you safe. "Yahweh chose me; Yahweh called me; Yahweh gives me the words to speak; Yahweh keeps me safe."

Jeremiah's Re-Call

That would be a good note on which to conclude a consideration of Jeremiah. Yet it would be a false note, because it might in the end suggest something too easy. It is more appropriate to conclude by returning to a passage from Jeremiah's laments.

> Oh, no! My mother, why did you bear me,
> a man involved in strife and contention through the whole
>   land? ...
> Have I not interceded with you for the enemy
> when he was in trouble and distress?
> Yahweh, remember me, attend to me,
> avenge me on my persecutors!
> You are slow to anger, but do not let me be taken.
> Consider the insults I bear on your account.
> Your words came, and I accepted them;
> your words were my joy, the delight of my heart,
> because you had made me your own....
> Why is my pain unceasing,
> my wound so severe, refusing to heal?
> You are just like a brook that fails,
> whose waters cannot be relied on (15:10,11,15,16,18).

"Before you were born, I set you apart"? *My mother, why did you bear me?* "I will be with you to keep you safe?" *Why is my pain unceasing, my wound so severe, refusing to heal?* "I have put my words in your mouth?" Yes, indeed, *your words came, and I accepted them; your words were my joy, the delight of my heart.* But their message does not come true: *You are just like a brook that fails, whose waters cannot be relied on.* In this lament Jeremiah seems to take up each element in his memory of his call to be a prophet, and repudiate it. He systematically tears to pieces the account of his call to Yahweh's service.

We may at this point note a contrast between Jeremiah and Jesus. Jesus does not go back on God's call. In Gethsemane he does question it, but he always accepts it. Jeremiah is more like Jesus Christ Superstar, who accepts God's call because, as he puts it, "You hold all the cards." There is something closer to resignation or compulsion there. The tortured surrender of Jeremiah or Jesus Christ Superstar contrasts with the willing acceptance of God's will by the Jesus of the Gospels, who can walk the tightrope of querying God's will without going back on his commitment to it.

Jeremiah and Jesus also differ in their attitude to their earthly enemies. Both pray for forgiveness for their persecutors. But here Jeremiah also prays for their punishment. In itself that is not wrong; prayer for justice to be done is prayer for God's will to be done. But the matter seems to have become one of personal vengeance: *avenge me on my persecutors.* Jeremiah, in the end, breaks. It should not surprise us; he *is* only a man. We will not make the mistake of pretending that we would have done better.

If Jeremiah's going back on his call highlights the difference between himself and Jesus, it also obscures the distinction between the true and the false prophet, which we considered above. Perhaps the true and the false prophet are in the end theoretical types. There is not a fixed collection of the one and a fixed collection of the other. Another reason why the line between false and true is difficult to draw is that a false prophet may speak an authentic word, and a true prophet can cease to

What makes someone a prophet?

be the channel of God's message. Perhaps there is no such thing as a true or a false prophet; there are only true and false prophecies. If so, then in this lament Jeremiah makes the transition from one to the other. He turns his back on God's calling and on God's word.

But as a true prophet can fall away, so a false prophet can return and be restored. He is not necessarily lost, even though he makes radical mistakes. The stories of Elijah and Jonah make that clear. But so does this story of Jeremiah's reaching breaking-point and of Yahweh's response to him on this occasion.

> Therefore Yahweh says,
> If you turn back, I will have you back
> to stand before me.
> If you utter what is valuable instead of what is worthless,
> you will be as my own mouth.
> They will have to come back to you,
> you will not have to go back to them.
> I will make you into a fortified wall of bronze before this
>   people.
> They will fight you, but not overcome you,
> for I will be with you to deliver you and to keep you safe.
> This is Yahweh's message (15:19-20).

Jeremiah has got out his prophetic credentials, torn them up, and trampled them in the mud, like a child angrily spurning the gift that was not what it wanted. But God responds like the parent who retrieves the spurned gift and puts it together again to show the child how it works and how it could be worth having after all. God in turn takes up the themes of Jeremiah's call and reaffirms them. "I am with you to keep you safe"? Yes, *I am with you to deliver you and to keep you safe.* "I have put my words in your mouth"? *Yes, you will be as my own mouth.* "I am making you a fortified city, an iron pillar, and bronze walls against Judah; they will fight you but not prevail over you"? Yes, that is all still true (15:20, compare 1:18-19).

But there is a condition attached. *If you turn back.... If you utter what is valuable instead of what is worthless.* The arms of love remain open; the commissioning hand remains raised. The call can always be renewed. God promises that there can still be forgiveness, usefulness, and success (15:19), that there can still be strength and protection (15:20), *if you turn back*—if your mouth (which in the previous verses has been used for Jeremiah's own words) becomes a vehicle for God's words again.

I have suggested previously that through his life I imagine Jeremiah lived with a tension between outward certainty and inner conflict. I suspect he also lived also with another tension (indeed it was part of his inner conflict), a tension between the experience of chapter 1 and the experience of chapter 15. The flesh ever called him to the outburst of chapter 15, but the spirit drew him back to the call from which he could not finally escape. It was a real tension. But the last word should be with the gracious, persisting, calling God. "I acknowledged you. I set you apart. I appointed you. You are to go to anyone to whom I send you, and to say anything that I tell you. I will be with you to keep you safe. I have put my words in your mouth." And "if you turn back, I will have you back to stand before me. If you utter what is valuable instead of what is worthless, you will be as my own mouth."

CHAPTER FIVE

The moment of fulfillment

The book of Jeremiah ends in a slightly puzzling way, with the unpleasant story of the last days of the reign of King Zedekiah. It is not only an unpleasant story, but also potentially a boring one if the reader knows the preceding books of the Old Testament, because it has already been told at the end of the books of Kings (2 Kings 25), at the end of the books of Chronicles (2 Chr. 36), and even earlier on in the book of Jeremiah (Jer. 39). If there is any chapter that could happily have been left out of the Bible, surely this is it? Why was it included?

The story recounts how Zedekiah rebelled against Nebuchadrezzar, like his brother Jehoiakim a decade previously. The Babylonian king came to put down the rebellion and laid siege to Jerusalem (52:3-5). Old Testament Jerusalem had a strong position. Not only was it on the ridge of a mountain range, but it was on a spur of this range, with the ground falling away sharply on three sides. It was thus difficult to capture from the east or the south or the west: an attacking army is climbing up a steep hill and the people at the top are dropping boulders on the attackers' heads. It is not this fact alone, however, that explains how Jerusalem could survive an eighteen-month siege. Half way through, the book of Jeremiah tells us earlier on, the Egyptians came to help Judah, as Zedekiah hoped, and Nebuchadrezzar had to go off to settle things with them (see Jer. 37). This no doubt gave the people chance to replenish their supplies.

But in due course Nebuchadrezzar returned, shortage of food became very severe in the city, and eventually there was no bread left at all (52:6). This unemotive phrase clearly describes a grim situation, which should perhaps remind us of those pictures from different African countries of refugees dying by the roadside and of babies who are just skin and bone. Indeed, in a way it was worse than this, as we learn from the poems in the book of Lamentations (five psalms belonging to the period of the exile). The level of human degradation was such that women were reduced to eating the flesh of their own children (see Lam. 2:20). It had happened before in a siege of Samaria (2 Kings 6:24-29). Perhaps people found themselves asking whether Nebuchadrezzar could do worse to them by capturing them than he had done by besieging them. Finally the gates were opened (52:7) and in rode Nebuchadrezzar.

No doubt Zedekiah and his soldiers had known they were in the greatest danger and they had taken flight, managing to find their way through the Babylonian lines down into the Arabah, the desert region that starts immediately east of Jerusalem and extends down the mountains to the oasis of Jericho and the Dead Sea. It is an area where Jews have often taken refuge; perhaps Zedekiah reckoned that now for a time they would have to become a guerrilla army, until the Babylonians tired of searching for them in the desert. But the Babylonians found Zedekiah and marched him to Nebuchadrezzar's headquarters in Syria. From there he was taken in humiliation to Babylon as another living proof of Nebuchadrezzar's might. But as a punishment for his disloyalty and to make sure that no-one ever contemplated putting him on a throne again—what use is a blind man as a king?—his sight was destroyed. Probably they

The moment of fulfillment

did it by searing his eyes with red-hot iron. The final image that he took with him to Babylon was his own sons' death. Zedekiah, the youngest son of Josiah, was a man of about forty. His sons will have been little boys or teenagers, but they were potential successors to his throne. So the last thing that his eyes beheld was the death of these boys. *The king of Babylon slew Zedekiah's sons before his eyes. He also slew all the nobles of Judah at Riblah. He blinded Zedekiah's eyes and bound him in chains. Thus the king of Babylon took him to Babylon and put him in prison until he died* (52:10-11).

The remainder of this closing chapter of Jeremiah describes the sack of Jerusalem itself. The temple, the palace, and people's homes were set on fire, and the walls of Jerusalem were demolished. The fittings and vessels of the temple (which are described in poignant detail) were appropriated. The chief priest and some other temple officials, as well as some military and political figures, were killed. Anyone else of any significance was taken off to Babylon. There is a tiny note of hope in the final paragraph, which relates how the already-exiled King Jehoiachin was released from prison by Nebuchadrezzar's son, Evilmerodach. But apart from that, it is a grim story.

So why is it in the Bible? One reason may be that it reflects the Bible's recognition of the tragic side to human existence. It acknowledges that human life is characterized by disaster and death, by calamity and grief, by misfortune and loss. Zedekiah was one of the younger of Josiah's sons. He was never destined to be king and he was not equipped for it. But circumstances took him to the throne. On the throne of Judah, he was not so much a really wicked king as a rather feeble one. The stories in the book of Jeremiah that involve him (see chs 32–35; 37–39) suggest that he wanted to follow the counsel of Jeremiah, recognizing it as both religious truth and political sense. But he lacked the moral strength to resist the heady courage of the generals urging him to go for independence and to throw off Babylonian rule. Consequently he was unable to avert calamity from Judah and indeed brought calamity on his family and on himself.

This is the tragedy of Zedekiah. It exemplifies the tragedy that often seems to characterize human life. We see people making misguided choices, decisions that clearly threaten calamity but that seem impossible to avert. We see it still on an ongoing basis in the Middle East, or in Northern Ireland, and we may be able to identify it in our own national life from time to time as we make decisions that fail to make sense morally or even pragmatically.

Now of course we do not need the Bible to tell us about these things; we know them too well without it. But we may note nevertheless that the Bible does describe this kind of world. Christianity is not a religion that hides from the realities of life; it faces up to them. Sometimes Christians do hide from these realities or behave as if life in its tragedy and calamity are nothing to do with God. We assume God is concerned only with prayer and church. But the world is God's world, and the Bible recognizes the element of tragedy about human experience and says that God is involved in it.

Thus the story of the fall of Jerusalem presupposes that history is in the control of the God of Israel. Even in this tragedy, with its human mistakes and its sin and evil, God's purpose is being worked out. *Jerusalem and Judah so angered the LORD that in the end he banished them from his sight; and Zedekiah rebelled against the king of Babylon* (52:3 NEB). It is striking how the two parts of that sentence fit together. God decided that enough was enough; the time to act had come. God's anger had to receive expression. But what happens is not that God sends an earthquake to destroy Jerusalem or that a flash of lightning from heaven consumes it. *Zedekiah rebelled against the king of Babylon;* and Zedekiah knew what he was doing. He made his decision and he put it into effect. Yet at the same time it was the working out of God's will. Nebuchadrezzar knew what he was doing. He did it for good political reasons. Yet unknown to him, he was Yahweh's servant, Jeremiah says (Jer. 25:9); it was Yahweh who brought him up against the Judeans, say the books of Chronicles (2 Chr. 36:17). People's own free decisions are the

The moment of fulfillment

means by which God's purpose is put into effect. It is thus God who controls history. God proves this by frustrating human purposes when necessary. After the fall of the city Zedekiah fled towards the Arabah, and there his troops scattered (Jer. 52:7-8). Yet even in that wilderness the Babylonians found him. How did that come about? Well, after all, "they had God, as it were, as their guide," comments John Calvin (*Commentary on the Book of Jeremiah*, Volume 4, p. 426). Nebuchadrezzar put an end to the rule of the Davidic line in Jerusalem, burned down the temple, took its vessels to Babylon, broke down the city's walls and deported its remaining worthwhile citizens to Babylon; but within 150 years there have been Davidic princes back in Jerusalem, the temple is rebuilt and functioning again, as many Judeans as wish to return are back, the city walls are rebuilt, and it is the Babylonian empire that is now only a figure in the history books. And this further reversal comes about because history is in the control of the God of Israel.

It is perhaps surprising, however, that this same history so often seems to bring trouble on Israel itself, and thus discredit on Yahweh's name. But this fact draws attention to another implication of the presence in the Bible of a story such as this one. It is that God has a *righteous* purpose to fulfill in history. *Jerusalem and Judah angered the LORD* (52:3). It is not that God is rather fickle and inexplicably irascible. It is that they *did what was wrong in the eyes of the LORD* (52:2 NEB). They ignored the Torah and the messages of prophets such as Jeremiah. They ignored Yahweh's standards of justice, morality, and mercy. They either placed a false trust in Yahweh, as if Yahweh were unconditionally committed to them forever, or they turned their backs on Yahweh and worshipped other gods.

The Old Testament (particularly Ezekiel) pictures God placed in a certain dilemma by this eventuality. Yahweh has taken the risk of making a commitment to this people and to their king. Yahweh's reputation and purpose are tied up with them. If he abandons them, he punishes himself. If he lets them off, he frustrates his own moral purpose. Neither a sinful people, nor a destroyed people, could reveal to the world a holy and loving God. On the one hand, he does banish them from his sight (52:3). But precisely because his purpose is to reveal himself to the world, this cannot be his last word. Indeed, Jeremiah has already told us that beyond calamity there will be restoration. He has made his surprising investment in real estate when the siege of Jerusalem was temporarily alleviated, though its eventual fall remained inevitable (see Jer. 32-33). That was a concrete expression of Jeremiah's commitment to the certainty that a time would come when land would be bought and sold again in the country that Nebuchadrezzar was bent on devastating. In the same context, Jeremiah speaks of the renewing of the broken covenant between Yahweh and Israel, of its renewing on a better and more permanent basis than before (Jer. 31:31-34; 32:36-41).

Again, the last chapter of Jeremiah speaks of the evil deeds of King Zedekiah and of his humiliation and disfiguring by Nebuchadrezzar (Jer. 52:2-3, 9-11). But Zedekiah is a prince of the line of David, that line to which God made his eternal commitment and of which the Messiah was to be born. Here, Calvin again comments, "Lying prostrate at the feet of a proud conqueror" is "a king... who was a type of Christ" (p. 428). This humiliation cannot be God's last word. Indeed, as with the new covenant, Jeremiah has already told us it is not. Zedekiah's own name means "Yahweh is my *righteousness*, my vindication." God has already promised that he is going to raise up for David's fallen tree a *righteous* branch, who will execute *righteousness* in the land, and who will be called "Yahweh-zidkenu" (23:5-6). The king is called "Yahweh is my righteousness"; but he does not live up to the name and must be cast off. But one day there will be a king worthy of the name, "Yahweh is our righteousness." The same *righteous* purpose of God that brings the fall of Jerusalem and the exile of Zedekiah, also guarantees the fulfillment of God's purpose of restoration in the future. Destruction is not God's *last* word to his people.

This leads us to a further insight on why this story appears in

The moment of fulfillment

the Bible, and more specifically on why it comes in this particular place, at the end of the book of Jeremiah (and not merely in the historical books). Why are we not told about the rest of Jeremiah's life? Why is it left to legends to tell us how he died?

The answer lies in the fact that the book of Jeremiah is not essentially about Jeremiah. It is about the word of God. The book itself begins the way other prophetic books do: *These are the words of Jeremiah.... Yahweh's word came to him...* (Jer. 1:1-2). It is a book about words. Even the stories are about what happens to God's *word*. They are accounts of how people respond to God's word, not merely to Jeremiah.

If it is right to look at the book as a whole in this way, then the final chapter after all constitutes an appropriate end to it. The chapter tells, in a quite matter-of-fact way, of how events turned out just as God had said. The word of God's prophet is proved right. Even though Jeremiah himself is not mentioned in this final chapter, it is the vindication of *his* ministry.

It thus also suggests that the other side of his word will be fulfilled. Jeremiah's message was, "Yahweh will break this covenant and make a new one; he will depose this king and bring forth a new branch from the stump of Jesse." If the first half of the declaration is fulfilled, the latter half will be, too.

But what is the proof of this? *The word of our God endures forever* (Isa. 40:8). That statement of faith takes us from the book of Jeremiah to the book of Isaiah. Although we can listen to people's numbed response to the fall of Jerusalem and to the exile in Lamentations and in Psalm 137, the prophecies in Isaiah 40–55 also reflect that response.

> The path I tread is hidden from Yahweh.
> My cause has passed out of God's notice (40:27).
>
> Yahweh has abandoned me.
> The Lord has forgotten me (49:14).

> These two things have happened to you—
> who is there to grieve with you?
> Devastation and destruction, famine and sword—
> how can I comfort you? (51:19).

> All humanity is grass,
> they last as long as a wild flower.
> Grass withers, flowers fade,
> when Yahweh's breath blows on them.
> Certainly the people are grass (40:6-7).

The prophet shares these feelings as a Judean in exile, but describes them as the background for a new word from God that brings good news to people who have no comforter because they have been abandoned and forgotten by God. "Yes, you have been under God's judgment," Second Isaiah says, "But that's over now. Yahweh's face had turned away from you, but now Yahweh has come back."

> Comfort, comfort my people, says your God.
> Encourage Jerusalem, proclaim to it:
> its bondage is over, its penalty is paid;
> it has received from Yahweh's hand
> full punishment for its sins (40:1-2).

The prophet is commissioned to preach to a people whose faith is burnt out, whose morale is gone, whose hope is extinguished, and to tell such a people that their God is alive, does care, and is about to return to them. They said, *The path I tread is hidden from Yahweh, my cause has passed out of God's notice.* Second Isaiah replied, *Do you not know? Have you not heard? Yahweh is the eternal God.... He gives strength to the weary...* (40:27-31). They said, *The Lord has forgotten me.* Yahweh declared, *Can a woman forget the baby she feeds...? Even if these should forget, I will not forget you* (49:14-15). They said there was no-one to comfort them in their distress (51:19). Yahweh declared,

The moment of fulfillment

Comfort my people (40:1). They said they felt like grass scorched by the sun. He replied, *Yes, the grass withers, the flowers fade; but the word of our God endures for ever* (40:6-8). "The word of our God" is the declaration of commitment God has made to the people, God's promises to them. This is the message of Second Isaiah in the exile, concerned to meet God's people where they are, to lift their spirits, to build up their faith, to re-establish their morale, to restore their hope, to rebuild their commitment. The prophetic message is that God has not cast them off, has not finished with them. The moment has come when God is restoring them. *The mouth of Yahweh has spoken* (40:5).

PART TWO

Isaiah 40–55

He said to me…
"I shall appoint you as a light to the nations"
(Isaiah 49:3,6)

CHAPTER SIX

The chosen servant
Isaiah 41:1-20

So the Isaiah of the exile is called to bring a message of comfort and challenge to the Judean community that has been in Babylon for a half a century—most of whom, therefore, have never known any thing else. In bringing this message, one of the prophet's recurrent themes is the motif of the servant of Yahweh, an idea that appears in most of chapters 40–55 (see 41:8-9; 42:1,19; 43:10; 44:1,2,21,26; 45:4; 48:20; 49:3-6; 50:10; 52:13; 53:11). It is a key motif that expresses some of the most important aspects of the chapters' message.

If asked whom the prophet meant by the servant of Yahweh, most Christians would reply that the expression refers to Jesus Christ, and this is certainly the major thrust of the New Testament's references to passages from Isaiah about the servant. Even in the New Testament, however, the possibility of other views is recognized. The question is raised by the Ethiopian official who was reading the most detailed of the passages about the servant (Isa. 52:13–53:12) when he was met by Philip the evangelist (see Acts 8:26–40). Puzzled by what he is reading, the Ethiopian's first thought is that the prophet is speaking of himself—and Paul refers 49:1–6 to himself (see Acts 13:47). When we go back to Isaiah 40–55 itself, further, we find that the chapters' first reference to the servant explicitly identifies the servant as Israel (Isa. 41:8–10).

These three possibilities—that the servant is Jesus, that it is the prophet, that it is Israel—all have their supporters today. In my view, there is truth in all of them. The servant calling belongs first to Israel as the people of God. It cannot fulfill it, however, and God calls the prophet to be this servant. But the chapters imply that in its ultimate dimensions the role of the servant embodies a vision that goes beyond the prophet's calling. The Christian finds it fulfilled in Jesus, but also sees it as passed on by him to those who follow him and those who claim to represent him.

But this is to anticipate a picture that develops only as the chapters unfold. We must begin with Israel.

Reasons for dismay

> But you are Israel my servant,
> Jacob whom I chose,
> the descendants of Abraham my friend.
> I took you from the ends of the earth,
> I called you from its farthest corners."
> I said to you "You are my servant,
> I chose you, I did not reject you.
> Do not look about in fear,
> I am with you, I am your God.
> I strengthen you, I help you,
> I support you with my right hand; it sees to what is right.
> (41:8-10).

The heart of the opening message about the servant lies here. "Don't be afraid, Israel. You are my chosen servant. I am alongside you."

These verses themselves, and their context, suggest several reasons why the Judeans in exile might have been afraid. They

The chosen servant

would have been naturally fearful about world affairs. They were living at a time of international unrest, a time when the Persian king, Cyrus, was beginning to rampage around the Middle East. He is trampling kings under foot, making them like dust with his sword, advancing from city to city so fast his feet seem scarcely to touch the ground (41:2–3). It is a time of world uncertainty, when no-one can be quite sure what will happen next, like living in Eastern Europe in 1939 or 1944, or like living in the Middle East today. The prophet describes how the people of Babylon itself were responding to this situation:

> The coastlands have seen this, and are afraid.
> The ends of the earth tremble with fear.
> They have come and assembled.
> Everyone helps their neighbor
> and says to their mate, "Take courage."
> The craftsman encourages the goldsmith,
> the man who beats out the metal with the hammer
>   encourages the one who strikes the nails,
> saying of the solder, "That's good,"
> and fastening it with nails so that it will not move (41:5-7).

It is a pathetic picture of desperate attempts to cope when history seems to be collapsing. People are naturally afraid and dismayed because of world affairs. They naturally respond by manufacturing their own solutions.

What is Second Isaiah's response? What is the word of Yahweh in such a situation? It is striking that the prophet does not speak as though this historical crisis is outside God's purpose. One might not have been surprised if the purported word of Yahweh had asserted, "Yes, the tyrant Cyrus, Yahweh's enemy, is advancing and will cause terrible trouble, but you must stand firm and believe that God will protect his people." This was in fact approximately what the Babylonian priests would say about their God. The prophet of Yahweh does not say that world affairs are going the opposite way to what God wants, but that he will nevertheless deliver you. Rather, like Jeremiah, the prophet declares that world events are working out in exactly the way Yahweh wants. It is for this reason that Yahweh's people have no reason to fear. God is not just someone to protect them from crises, but someone who brings about crises. Yahweh is the Lord of history.

The prophet makes this point by challenging people in general to give some explanation of where Cyrus came from. Often in these chapters, he is nominally addressing the whole world. But in reality, it is the Judeans themselves who are encouraged to think.

> Keep silence before me, you coastlands.
> Let the peoples summon up new strength,
> let them come forward and speak.
> Let us meet together to give judgment.
> Who roused one from the east,
> one whom a righteous purpose greets at every step?
> He gives nations over to him,
> he subdues kings.
> His sword makes them like dust,
> his bow makes them like straw blowing in the wind.
> He pursues them and passes on from success to success,
> his feet do not touch the road.
> Who acted, who did it,
> summoning the course of history from the beginning?
> I, Yahweh, I am the first,
> and I am with the last. I am the one (41:1-4).

It is Yahweh, the God of Israel, who is bringing about this historical crisis. It is therefore entirely natural for the Babylonians to panic (41:5). But it is not natural for the Judeans to do so, because the same God who is the Lord of historical crises is the God who promises to look after Israel. The historical crises are part of God's gracious will. The people can relax when the world seems to be falling apart, because they know who is making it fall apart; they know who is in control. *The Babylonians tremble; but you are Israel my servant, Jacob whom I chose...*

The chosen servant

Do not look about in fear, I am with you (41:8,10). The Babylonians are in a panic because of somebody coming from the east, but you are the children of one who came from the east, you are *the descendants of Abraham my friend. I took you from the ends of the earth, I called you from its farthest corners. I said to you "You are my servant," I chose you, I did not reject you* (41:8-9). The Babylonians are dismayed at the victories of Cyrus: but your God gives him those victories, they are the righteous achievements of God's right hand, active on your behalf (41:10). The Babylonians desperately look to each other for help and strength like drunks hoping to find support by leaning on each other: but Yahweh strengthens you, Yahweh upholds you (41:10). The people of God have no reason to be fearful or dismayed about world affairs, because the Lord of world affairs is their Lord and they are this God's servants.

The exiles would also feel a natural fear of the people they had to live among. It was the usual Jewish story: they formed an alien element in a hostile environment. They did not really belong in the country they lived in. Indeed, at this point in time, they had not at all chosen to go to this particular place. They had been taken there by force as prisoners of war and dumped in a refugee camp like Arab refugees in the Middle East today. They were not popular with the people they had to live among. Physically, indeed, they were reasonably well off. They had their own communities, places of meeting and leadership. They were sufficiently comfortable for many to prefer to stay there when the chance to go home came. But nevertheless they formed an alien element in a hostile environment and it would be natural to be afraid of those they had to live among.

But it is these opponents who are in a state of panic over the advance of Cyrus, it is these who have no way of coping with the way world affairs are unfolding. So here is the word of Yahweh in relation to that need.

> All those who rage at you will know disappointment and shame.

Those who quarrel with you will vanish into nothing.
You will look for those who attack you, but not be able to find them.
Those who do battle with you will cease to exist at all
(41:11-12).

In these two verses the hostility of their enemies is described in sharper and sharper terms. First it is annoyance (11a), then opposition (11b), then attack (12a), finally war (12b). This is not just vivid imagination. The Babylonians have actually behaved in such ways in relation to Israel in the years that led up to the exile. The prophet assumes (as no doubt the exiles assume) that the Babylonians are not going to change character overnight as Cyrus advances; perhaps rather the opposite.

The prophet is quite realistic about the peril the Judeans are in and does not underestimate the danger that comes from those they live among. That can be faced openly, if one knows that God is going to deal with it. Second Isaiah knows that the sharper their opposition, the more complete will be their downfall. Thus, at the same time as the description of their enemies' hostility gets sharper and sharper, the promise of how they will be dealt with gets more and more devastating. First they will be put to shame (11a), then they will disappear (11b), then you will not be able to find them (12a), finally they cease to exist at all (12b).

We ought perhaps to recall whom the prophet is speaking of. It is the mighty Babylonian empire, the people who built the ziggurats and the hanging gardens of Babylon, the people who had twice besieged and conquered Jerusalem, and who now held the leading Judeans in exile. Of them the prophet says, "Do not assume they are going to get more friendly: the coming crisis is likely to have the opposite effect. Nevertheless, even as their hostility increases, you will see them put to shame, vanish, disappear, cease to exist. The bigger they are, the harder they fall."

The prophet knows this, because of knowing who Israel's God is. *For I, Yahweh, your God, I hold you by the hand* (41:13).

The chosen servant

Remember who Yahweh is? Yahweh is the creator of the ends of the earth (40:28: see 40:12-31 generally). Yahweh is the Lord of history from beginning to end who is also active in present world affairs (41:4). This is *the one who says to you, "Do not be afraid, I will help you"* (41:13). Again we recall the prophet's description of the threatened Babylonians desperately trying to prop each other up as the crisis point draws near (41:5-7), and we hear Yahweh saying to the people, "Do not be afraid of those around you. *I* will be *your* help."

Further, the exiles would naturally be dismayed at the obstacles that lay between them and their return to their own land. This seems to be the point of the reference to their being confronted by mountains and hills (41:14-16). The prophet has spoken earlier of mountains and hills: *every valley will rise up, and every mountain and hill lie flat* (40:4). There the words certainly alluded to the obstacles that hindered Yahweh's return to Jerusalem. The prophet declares that those obstacles would be removed. As a freeway carves its way across a landscape, scything its path through the hills and supported by embankments over the valleys, so Yahweh's highway will take Yahweh back to Jerusalem. And the people will travel with him (40:10-11). Their exile is coming to an end. Yahweh is going home; and they are going home too.

But the obstacles to the people getting home were huge, indeed mountain-sized. The opposition of the Babylonians, which we have already referred to, is one such. Another is the sheer distance and the physical barriers in the way. It is not primarily mountain-country but desert, yet nevertheless a huge obstacle separating Babylon from Jerusalem. Another obstacle would be the sheer perversity of the exiles themselves. When the gospels speak of mountains and valleys being leveled before the Lord comes (see especially Luke 3:1-14), it is moral obstacles to God's working that they have in mind. Huge barriers seemed to hinder the people's getting back home; mountains and hills dismayed them. That was the worm's eye-view: Israel felt exactly like a tiny worm before them (41:14).

The prophet would grant that a worm can make little impression on a mountain. But God promises to turn Israel from a worm into a threshing sledge (41:15). A threshing sledge was a wooden platform with bits of iron or stone set in the bottom. After the corn had been cut and collected together for threshing, the farmer sat or stood on his threshing sledge while his oxen pulled it back and forward, round and round, over the corn, until it was all cut up into tiny bits. Then he could fork it into the air so that the wind would carry the chaff away. Now, says Yahweh,

> I am making you into a threshing-sledge,
> a new one, studded with teeth.
> You will be able to thresh the mountains and crush them,
> and make the hills like chaff.
> You will be able to winnow them
> so that the wind can take them and the storm scatter them
> (41:15-16).

The obstacles to going home look like mountains. But the Judeans will overcome them as easily as the farmer crushes the grain and disposes of the chaff. No matter how huge are the obstacles that stand between the place where God's people are and the place of blessing where God purposes to take them, these obstacles cannot withstand God's plan to fulfill such promises to them.

What are the grounds for the prophet's conviction of this? On what basis are people to believe such promises? *I am the one who helps you,* says Yahweh once again. *Your restorer is the holy one of Israel* (41:14). Those two descriptions of God are very important; it is in them that the justification for confidence lies. The prophet speaks in the name of "the holy one of Israel." This theme, as we have noted above, runs through the whole book of Isaiah. It goes back to Isaiah's own vision of God, exalted in glory (Isaiah 6). There the seraphim acknowledged him as the ultimate holy one: "*Holy, holy, holy is Almighty Yahweh*" (6:3). Overhearing their worship, Isaiah of Jerusalem took this as a

The chosen servant

keynote of his message. Israel's God is the holy one. But Israel had failed him, indeed had rebelled against him. Therefore as the holy one, Yahweh will punish Israel. That is Isaiah's message in the eighth century.

With the exile the calamity came. The holy one had demonstrated the divine holiness by this act of punishment. Now the message is to be different. Yahweh is still the holy one of Israel, still attached to Israel, still faithful to the commitment made to it. Being the holy one of Israel was a threat to it when it was in a state of sin. But now in its state of need it is a reassurance.

This point is made explicit by declaring that this holy one is Israel's *restorer*. Here is another word with a long history. It means a close relative, someone who belongs to your fairly immediate family. Such a person had obligations to you: if you were in need, such a person had to help you. For instance, if you got into debt and had to sell your land, or even to sell yourself into slavery to pay the debt, your close relatives were under moral obligation to come to your aid. Two near English words are "next-of-kin" and "guardian"—the word, that is, suggests a member of your family who steps in to look after your interests when you cannot look after yourself.

So, the prophet says, you can be sure that Yahweh will fulfill those promises to you and that the huge obstacles that cut you off from your homeland can be overcome because the holy one of Israel is your next-of-kin, your guardian. You belong to the same family. Yahweh is the close relative who steps in to look after your interests in this situation where you cannot look after yourself. So again, you have no reason to look about in fear.

Yet another reason for the exiles to feel dismay is expressed in a further paragraph (41:17-20). It reveals a further aspect of how Israel feels: poor and needy, seeking water but finding none, parched with thirst. Again, the picture takes up an aspect of life in the Middle East. In Britain, sun is good news, rain is no news. In May or June as summer approaches people's spirits lift, in October or November as winter draws near they probably flag.

In the Middle East, as in Southern California, it is the other way round. In summer the sun bakes the land dry and kills nearly everything that grows. People look forward to October or November and to the rain, because it means the revival of nature. If the rains fail, nature stays lifeless. The crops fail. The animals die of thirst.

That experience of baking drought every summer (and of drought at other times, if people were unfortunate) suggests a way people in the Bible, particularly in the Psalms, describe themselves when they are in need. We are like the land parched for lack of rain. As Ezekiel puts it in his vision of the valley of dry bones, "Our bones are dried up, our hope has gone; we are as good as dead" (Ezek. 37:11 JB). We have been abandoned. We have nowhere to find refreshment or renewal.

Here is Second Isaiah's response to that lament.

> The poor and needy are looking for water, and there is none;
> their tongues are parched with thirst.
> I, Yahweh, will answer them;
> as the God of Israel I will not abandon them (41:17).

"You think it is all over, but you are wrong. You have abandoned belief in Yahweh, the God of Israel. You doubt whether it is worth pleading with him about the situation any more. So you feel like the Judean wilderness, those bare sun-baked slopes where a person can get lost and die of heat and thirst within a few miles of civilization. But imagine those bare hills suddenly irrigated, watered, planted, forested. I could do that for your lives."

> I can open up rivers in land that is bare
> and fountains in the middle of valleys.
> I can make the wilderness into a lake
> and land into springs of water.
> In the wilderness I can place cedar trees,
> acacias, myrtles, olive trees.
> In the desert I can put junipers,

pines and cypresses side by side (41:18-19).

The feeling that you are cut off from all sources of renewal, that everything has run dry, is not reason for dismay, for Yahweh remains able to open up springs in the desert, able to bring refreshment to places that are dry and parched.

The underlying fear

There, then, are the pressures that drive the community to the ground: the world affairs that threaten it; the attitude of people around it; the obstacles that confront it; the personal needs within it. But there is one other cause of dismay that lies just under the surface of these feelings. We have come close to it in passing just now, for we have noted that God says, *I will not abandon them* (41:17). That promise hints at a further and most fundamental reason for the exiles' dismay. They were afraid that, whereas they used to be able to turn to Yahweh when world events threatened them or people attacked them or obstacles confronted them or personal needs depressed them, now they can do that no longer. Yahweh himself has abandoned them. The fall of Jerusalem and the dragging years in exile make that quite clear. Yahweh has finished with them. This is why fear, referred to three times in five verses (41:10,13,14), has replaced faith. They are afraid, not merely of the Persians or the Babylonians. They are afraid of the future, afraid of life itself without Yahweh, afraid of Yahweh, indeed, who they know still exists (people in the ancient world never seemed to doubt the existence of their gods) but who now seems to be permanently against them instead of being for them.

There is another hint of this feeling in the paragraph about drought and refreshment (41:17-20). Sometimes one of our children would come to my wife or me and say, "Will you read me a book?" or "Will you take us swimming?" or "Can I have an ice cream?" At other times (perhaps because we had already said no) they would mooch around in a dejected way talking under their breath to no-one in particular. "I wish there was someone to read me a book." "I wish we could go swimming." "I'm starving." There is an important difference between those two ways of speaking. One is a request addressed to a person who could actually meet it, and there is evidently reckoned to be a fair chance that he or she will. The other presupposes (rightly or wrongly) that he or she is not interested or is bound to say no, and it is really a lament at the unsatisfactoriness of life rather than an actual request.

Adults in their own way lament the unsatisfactoriness of life, too; no doubt, we learned to do it when we were children. We bemoan whatever is getting on top of us, bemoan it to ourselves; we can talk only to ourselves about it, because there is no-one else to tell about it, is there?

Apparently what Israel was doing was not so very different from this. *The poor and needy are seeking water and finding none and their tongue is parched with thirst....* It is all very indirect, like the children mooching around the living room resentful of some deprivation but knowing it is no use trying to interest the parents in it. The community is not really praying; it is just complaining out loud, because it no longer believes God is interested. God responds, nevertheless: *I will answer them.* The people's deepest need is for a reassurance of God's concern about it. Its morale has sunk back to the point it reached in its time in Egypt (see Exod. 2:23-24). There *the Israelites groaned under their bondage, and cried out.* There, too, it was no prayer; they lacked the resources any longer to lift their eyes Godwards. They could only lament their affliction. But nevertheless *their cry under bondage came up to God. God heard their groaning....* God was still bending an ear downwards. God took note of their distress and acted. The biggest challenge for the Isaiah of the exile, too, is to convince people that God is still listening and still cares.

Now it is in this connection that he reminds them that as Jacob-Israel they are Yahweh's servant. *I said to you, "You are my servant." I chose you, I did not reject you* (41:9). The fear that Yahweh has forsaken them underlies all their other fears. So the

The chosen servant

assurance that Yahweh has not abandoned them, and will not, underlies all the prophet's other promises.

"You are my chosen servant." The idea of being God's servant makes its first appearance in these prophecies as a reassurance for Jacob-Israel regarding its status with God. Yahweh is committed to it, chose it, entered into a relationship with it, and will not terminate the relationship. "You are my chosen servant. You have no reason to give up prayer, no reason to give in to fear."

Fear is one of the most elemental and basic of our human feelings in our lost state. Adam and Eve hiding in the garden, Cain terrified at being alone in the world, the people who half-built the city of Babel with its tower because they were afraid, Abraham fearful lest the Pharaoh kills him because he fancies Sarah: fear is a basic human emotion.

Of course fear should not be seen as essentially sinful. There is a right fear of God that we will keep even in heaven. There is a right fear of danger, crises, and challenges, that stops one from being foolhardy and encourages one to apply oneself to the task in hand. At another extreme, fear can come to possess a person's whole personality. Healthy apprehension that encourages revision before examinations becomes a paralyzing panic that makes work impossible. A prudent concern about germs becomes an irrational phobia that makes a person never cease washing the hands. Most of us are not afflicted by that. Yet we do fall into the kinds of anxiety the exiles felt. Humanly speaking, both their fears of world events and of people around, and their dismay at the obstacles that confronted them and at their own personal needs, were entirely rational. Humanly speaking, it was an appropriate response to a fearful set of circumstances.

But these human evaluations are confronted by the "gospel." The prophet uses this expression (40:9) in speaking of good news being brought to the exiles: the good news is that God is working out a purpose through world events, that God can deal with people who oppose the exiles, that God can remove the obstacles that separate the people of God from their destiny, that God can bring refreshment to places that are dry and parched.

When the people of God are in a situation where, humanly speaking, fear is the appropriate response, what God does is to make promises to them. That is all, at first. They are left in the situation, and left with the words that claim that "humanly speaking" is not all there is. They are challenged to let fear give way to trust because of these promises. If they do, then the place of fear can be a place of growth.

Thus rejoicing and glorying in Yahweh can replace fear. That is a final point made by this section of Isaiah's collected prophecies. Because he is going to do all this,

> You can rejoice in Yahweh,
> in the holy one of Israel you can glory (41:16).

The prophet's concern is that the good news of restoration should not merely be a comfort to the community, but should also lead to a return movement of praise and worship from them to God. This is the final aim, that God may have the glory. If they were to enjoy God's blessings and not give God the glory, then an important aspect of the point of the whole thing would be lost.

It is on this note that the whole section actually ends: not merely with the praise of Israel, but with the praise of the world. When God makes the wilderness of Israel's life into a green oasis, the ultimate aim is

> that people may see and acknowledge,
> may give heed and understand,
> that it is Yahweh's hand that has done this,
> it is the holy one of Israel who has created it (41:20).

CHAPTER SEVEN

The faithful servant
Isaiah 41:21-42:17

So Israel enjoys the privilege, the status, and the position of Yahweh's servant. The prophet goes on to describe what it means to be God's servant and what God's servant is called to, in what amounts to a job-description for the servant of Yahweh. It is the calling Israel was supposed to fulfill.

The job-description is contained in two prophecies that are now juxtaposed (42:1-4, 5-9). The first (1-4) describes God's servant. It talks about him. The second (5-9) addresses God's servant. It talks to him. The actual term "servant" does not appear in the second passage, but it seems to be referring to the same person as do the previous verses. The two passages are two accounts of how God commissions the servant, one addressed to other people, the other to him. But they are parallel in content, and similar themes recur.

Both begin with a kind of recap. *Here is my servant...* (42:1). The prophet describes Yahweh's servant in the same terms that appeared earlier. "You remember the servant we were speaking of before—the one *whom I support* (see 41:10), *the one I chose* (see 41:8), *the one in whom I delight*." These last words have not come previously, though the idea of Israel as the one "on whom God's favor rests" (cf. C. R. North, *The Second Isaiah*, p. 37) was fundamental to chapter 41.

There is a similar recap when Yahweh begins to speak directly to the servant (42:6): *I am Yahweh.* Remember how *I called you* (see 41:9) *with a righteous purpose* (see 41:10). *I took you by the hand* (see 41:9). *I kept you.* Again, these words have not come before; but they summarize 41:8-20. The fact that "righteousness" in 42:6 recaps 41:10 is not apparent in the modern English translations, but the Hebrew word generally translated "victorious" in 41:10 is the same as the one translated "righteous" in 42:6. The idea is that God's righteousness is not something abstract and inactive. It makes God get involved in the world giving victory to the cause of right. So both verses refer to this righteousness of God that is active in the world seeing that what is right wins the victory.

So Yahweh begins these two prophecies by recalling the position already given to this servant. He servant is loved by God, chosen by God, called by God, taken by the hand by God, upheld by God, kept by God. The message of comfort that the exiles needed is reasserted. But at this point in Isaiah 40–55 this is only a resume of previous words. What the prophet has to go on to say is more demanding than those words of comfort. The earlier words spoke of the commitment Yahweh makes to the servant, promising to be faithful to him and not to abandon him. Now Yahweh raises the question of the commitment expected of this servant. Is Yahweh's servant going to be faithful to Yahweh? Or is his servant going to abandon Yahweh?

To be chosen and called by God has as its object not just that one can enjoy basking in the sunshine of God's love. One can do that; but the experience is intended then to give to the people of God new resources and new strength with which to serve God. God is committed to them. Are they committed to God? So in these two paragraphs the prophet sets up a vision of what God's servant is called to be, unfolding what God's idea was in loving and choosing and calling, in taking and keeping and upholding.

The faithful servant

What the servant is called to do

I have put my spirit on him, he will bring my government to the nations (42:1). *I have made you a covenant to the people, a light to the nations* (42:6).

The servant is to be the means whereby Yahweh brings to humankind in general God's government, a covenant relationship, illumination.

These declarations have their background in passages earlier in Isaiah. Isaiah looks forward (see Isa. 2:2-5) to a day when nations and peoples will flock to Yahweh to learn of his ways by hearing his law (as in 42:4). Their strife with one another will end when he exercises government in the affairs of the nations (as in 42:1,3,4: God brings just government, authoritative decisions concerning the affairs of the nations). Isaiah closes that prophecy by encouraging Israel itself, having received God's laws, to walk in this light (compare 42:6). Subsequently (see 11:1-10), Isaiah speaks of a new David on whom the spirit of Yahweh will rest (compare 42:1), so that he will have the wisdom to exercise government (the same word as in 42:1,3,4 again) in a way that is fair and faithful (compare 42:3).

So the world is seen as in a state of chaos and disarray. The nations have no assured relationship with God. They are in the dark as to how their lives should be lived. God wants to bring the order that his just government makes possible. The word for "government" is often translated "judgment," but this "judgment" is not a negative thing, but the sorting out of rights and wrongs to make true life possible. God wants to enter into a relationship with the nations that they can rely on, a covenant relationship like the relationship between God and Israel. God wants to give them the light of revelation.

Indeed, the nations apparently realize that. The *coastlands* (perhaps the areas on the Mediterranean coastline, perhaps countries the other side of the Mediterranean—but they stand here for the gentiles in general) *are waiting for God's teaching*, for the message that the servant will bring them (42:4). The servant brings Torah (usually translated "law"): the statement makes it clear that God's "law" is not something burdensome, and the Old Testament does not see it as such. It is a gift. Torah means much more than a collection of laws. It covers teaching in general. God's "law" is God's revelation, God's word. Thus those who know God's "law" love it, rejoice in it, and enthuse over it (as Psalms 19 and 119 show); and those who do not know it are looking forward to discovering it.

They may not be doing so consciously, of course. In order to make life livable, people often have to hide from facing up to what they lack. They evade the admission that they have so little clue regarding what life means, where the world is going, and what their own existence is about. But the prophet presupposes that they are waiting (subconsciously, if not consciously) for someone to tell them the answers to these questions.

The servant's job is to make that possible by bringing God's government, God's covenant, God's light. Precisely how he does that is not here explained, though an earlier passage we referred to (Isa. 2) offers some suggestions. One way Israel will bring light to the world is by letting God's light flood through its own life. Isaiah had urged his hearers, "Let us walk in Yahweh's light" (2:5). It makes it clear that people can have a covenant relationship with God by enjoying that relationship itself. This is how the original promise to Abraham was to work. God would bless Abraham in a spectacular way to show what he could do for someone (see Gen. 12:1-3). If Israel lets God's light fill its life, this will make it a beacon that attracts the nations to it. It is then that the nations will flock to Jerusalem, knowing that this is where God's truth can be learned and God's government obtained. If people want matters sorted out, they will come to the God of Israel. God's people are expected thus to attract others to their God. Zechariah expresses the point beautifully a few years later: "Ten foreigners will come to one Jew and say, 'We want to share in your destiny, because we have heard that God is with you'" (Zech. 8:23 GNB).

The servant brings Yahweh's light to the nations by attracting

The faithful servant

them to Yahweh. He does not seem to be pictured as going out to tell the world about Yahweh. After all, the sun does not bring light to the earth by coming to the earth, but by staying where it is and shining. It is striking how little reference there is in the Old Testament to anything that one might call "missionary activity." It is not that the Old Testament assumes that Yahweh the God of Israel is not the God of the whole world or is not interested in the whole world. It is rather that it believes that the way the world is to be won is not by hard-sell proselytizing but by attracting people. Israel is to show in its life what God can do with a people, and thereby to invite them to seek him. Ultimately, indeed, it is not Israel that has to do this. It is God who does it through Israel. Israel has only to be available.

If the church now reckons to take on the role of God's means of reaching the world, then it has to accept this insight from Isaiah. It is particularly relevant when one considers the church's relationship with Israel itself. Christians would love to see Jews recognize that Jesus is their Messiah. But the church in its relationship with Judaism over the centuries has not manifested the light of God in its life. There is such a backlog of darkness in us that it is impossible for us to claim stridently that we have the truth. Jews may reasonably refuse to believe that the Messiah has come when they do not find a messianic people, cannot see the Messiah reigning in justice, and cannot perceive God's government, God's covenant grace, or God's light in those who claim to stand for it.

It would be a mistake to swing from one extreme to another and suggest that all we have to do is sit here and let people be drawn to us. Jesus did commission his people to go out into the world, and it was in connection with this active task that Paul picked up the motif of the servant bringing light to the world (Acts 13:47). Nevertheless, the servant people of God is called to accept the challenge to let the light of God's revelation shine in its own life.

How the servant is called to act

How is the servant to go about his task?

> He will not snap a broken reed,
> he will not snuff out a flickering flame (42:3).

Here are two ways of talking about violent death: it is like a reed being snapped, or like a flame being put out (this metaphor reappears in 43:17). We are to imagine people who are alive, but afflicted and oppressed, and we are to imagine a reed that is not actually snapped off, but is bent and bruised, or a candle that is not actually out, but is very low. People do not try to mend broken reeds; if a reed bends in someone's way, it gets trampled on. People do not take the flickering stub of a candle to read by; they snuff it out and light a new one. That is how the world treats people, too. But Yahweh's servant does not snap off broken reeds; he binds them up and supports them. He does not quench flickering flames; he fans them to a blaze again.

> He'll never quench the smoking flax,
>   But raise it to a flame;
> The bruised reed He never breaks,
>   Nor scorns the meanest name
>   (Isaac Watts' paraphrase, quoted by C. R. North,
>   *The Second Isaiah*, p. 109).

In these chapters of Isaiah, two contrasting attitudes to the nations appear. Sometimes the gentiles are seen as willful idolaters, opponents of Yahweh the only true God, guilty adversaries of Israel, and destined for punishment. In other passages, like the present one, they are seen as pitifully blind, weak, and helpless, as broken or fading. In as far as they are rebelling against God, they must be punished. But in as far as they are willing to acknowledge God they can open themselves to God's arms of love and to the arms of love that God's people extend.

The world is full of broken reeds and fading flames. Often

The faithful servant

they disguise themselves, present themselves as strong and aggressive: those are sometimes the most bruised ones. The servant of God is called to a ministry that does not break but binds, does not snuff them out but gently fans.

To put it another way, he is called

> to open blind eyes,
> to bring the captive out of prison,
> to bring those who live in the dark out of the dungeon (42:7).

There are two further powerful ways to describe not so much positive suffering such as persecution or pain or grief, as negative loss of well-being. To be blind is to be helpless, to be at a loss, to be incapable of finding your own way, to be unable to avoid dangers that are quite obvious to sighted people, to lose all independence. To blind someone is one of the most unpleasant punishments that can be imposed on them. We recall the fate of Zedekiah after Jerusalem was captured; the worst thing that the Babylonians could do to the rebel king was to blind him (Jer. 52:11). Perhaps he was still alive among the exiles, still a walking example of the deprivation of blindness.

Then, to be imprisoned is to lose freedom; that, in our culture at least, is one of the most fundamental human rights. Liberty! Prisoners have none. They can make no decisions. They can make no plans. They can take no initiatives. They sit and rot: physically, spiritually, mentally, emotionally. King Jehoiachin, the Babylonians' first royal hostage, had sat in a Babylonian prison for 37 years until he was released a few years previously. Perhaps he was still a walking reminder of what prison does to a man.

Here, however, blindness and imprisonment are two symbols of the circumstances of the nations. The task of the servant is to bring sight and freedom, because sight and freedom are the gifts of the God he serves.

What the servant needs to be wary of

The servant of Yahweh is called to minister to people whose persons are bruised, whose life is flickering, who can only cry pleadingly for help. It is easy to come to share the weaknesses of people you seek to minister to. As a young minister, I used to play soccer with a gang of rough teenagers. Whether or not I had any influence on them, they certainly taught me to play dirtier soccer! It is easy to be dragged down by the people we are seeking to help. That will not be the case with Yahweh's servant, however. *He will not cry out or lift up his voice, or make himself heard in the street* (42:3). The point of this assertion is not that the servant will not be an extroverted, loud-mouthed showman. The word for "cry out" is the one for a cry of distress. It appears in the exodus story, when the Israelites in Egypt *cried out for help, and their cry under bondage came up to God* (Exod. 2:23).

Israel is in bondage again, and in their distress in exile they cry out because of their affliction. The prophet implies an awareness of the fact that someone called to minister to people like that can come to be affected by their downcast-ness. The account of the prophet's commission implies a personal awareness of that danger. *"Preach,"* he heard the heavenly aide say (40:6—the verb "cry" is used here, too, in the English translations, but it is a different word from the one for crying in anguish; it means more generally to speak loudly). *"Preach what?"* The prophet replied. "We, your people, are withered like grass in the summer heat. What is the use of preaching to us?" The prophet felt what the people felt about the situation they were in. (See 40:6-7, where the response that begins in verse 6, "What shall I preach?" continues through to the end of verse 7; verse 8 is then the reply to it. See C. Westermann, *Isaiah 40–66*, p. 41.)

But the servant will be able to stay at a distance, in the right sense, from the afflicted people he has to minister to. So *he will not cry out*. Further, when he is involved in ministering to people who are broken and wavering (42:3), he himself *will not waver or break* (42:4). The verse repeats the words just applied to the people. They are broken and wavering, but *he will not waver or break until he has established [God's] government in the world* (42:4). The servant will not contract the weaknesses of those to whom he ministers. He has the personal resources to make a success of his calling. He has the staying power. But he needs to be wary of the pressures he will be under.

What there is to encourage him

In fulfilling his calling, he is not merely or finally dependent on people's awareness that they need God's truth, or on their broken and wavering state. Nor is he merely or finally dependent on his own resources; everything does not rest on him. His final encouragement lies in God himself.

He goes into God's world. The one who calls him is

> the one who created the heavens and stretched them out,
> who spread out the earth with all that comes from it,
> who gives breath to the people on it
> and life to those who live on it (42:5).

The servant is sent into God's world. That answers an objection the prophet, or the servant, might have been inclined to make. These messages often begin with God's self-description in terms such as these, and such introductions generally seem designed to forestall people's objections. They say to the hearer, as it were, when you listen to this message, if you find it difficult to accept, do not forget to take account of this.... Yahweh wants this servant to bring light to the nations. One objection to this might be, surely God is going to judge the nations? They are heathen. They do not acknowledge God. They have often persecuted God's people. They are responsible for our being in exile. Surely they are not to receive the light? Or again, supposing we agree that God may want to bless the nations in this way. Nevertheless, how can God expect a mere human servant to bring light to the nations? It is too big a task. We could not take that on.

Both those possible objections are forestalled by the reminder that Yahweh is the creator of heaven and earth, of the world and of humanity. That means on one hand that the God who is speaking these words is mighty enough to be able to see to the effecting of plans—any plans. If Yahweh declares the intention of using a servant in a certain way, that can certainly come about. After all, Yahweh made the universe, and has the power.

Further, being the creator of humanity, the one who breathes breath into each human being, implies caring for all those who live on earth. Having created them all, Yahweh is not interested in only a few. So the servant is given God's commission with regard to the world God created, and the creatures God cares about. That is the servant's first encouragement.

His second is that he goes into God's world because of God's summons. There is in the situation, then, all the potential that comes from being summoned by God. *I am Yahweh* (that self-declaration by God characteristically introduces some solemn statement). *I called you with a righteous purpose. I took you by the hand, I kept you* (42:6; compare 42:1). We have already considered those powerful descriptions of the special relationship between Yahweh and the servant. He is specially chosen, called, taken by the hand, endowed with God's spirit, upheld, kept. All those things are true of him because of his relationship with God; they are part of God's commitment to him. But they are very relevant as God issues this challenge regarding the servant's commitment to God and God's purpose. The servant is not acting on his own initiative or in his own strength, but in all the resources of his special calling and his special relationship.

His third encouragement is that God's summons relates to the recognition of God's own honor. *I am Yahweh. That is my name. My glory I give to no other, nor my praise to images* (42:8). The servant's task is to call the bluff of the Babylonian gods, and in principle that of human religion in general. But will it work? What if they laugh in his face? It will work because of Yahweh's own personal concern. Yahweh is not willing for recognition as God to go where it does not belong.

The faithful servant

But again, how do we know Yahweh is concerned for acknowledgment in this way, and that Yahweh is sufficiently powerful to achieve this? That question expresses precisely the exiles' doubts. The prophet answers it by claiming that the people can know God will fulfill this plan to be revealed, because God has fulfilled plans before. God has already acted in Israel's experience as one who speaks and then does things. God has demonstrated the ability to announce intentions and fulfill them. So if God is now announcing intentions to be fulfilled through this servant, the intentions will come to pass.

> Now that earlier things have clearly come about,
> I am declaring fresh things.
> Before they begin to happen
> I make them known to you (42:9).

The prophet refers to an important feature of Israel's experience of God throughout the time it was a political entity. Prophets often appeared, to declare what God had been doing, was doing, and was going to do. So, for instance, Isaiah of Jerusalem in the eighth century had involved himself in the political policy-making of Ahaz and Hezekiah. He had warned that the Assyrians would chastise Judah. He had declared that they, and other contemporary powers, would eventually see their own downfall. His words came true. Some were coming true before the exiles' own eyes: the Babylonian empire was in the midst of falling at the hand of the Medes, as Isaiah had said (see Isa. 13).

When people say after some event that they are not surprised, that they had thought it might happen, such a claim is less impressive than if beforehand they have gone on record and committed themselves regarding what they expect to take place. They can then point out subsequently that it has taken place as they said. It is this ability that the prophet is claiming for Yahweh here, and it points to a significant difference between Yahweh and the other gods.

That point was made by the paragraph that led into the passage about the servant (41:21-29: the chapter divisions in

Isaiah 40–55 are more often a hindrance than a help in understanding the prophet's message, and this last paragraph of chapter 41, for instance, is really the beginning of a new chapter). The paragraph again speaks of the dismay that world affairs might cause to the exiles and to the Babylonians. Earlier, the prophet had challenged the Babylonian gods regarding who is making these events occur (see 41:1-7). Here, however, the challenge concerns the different question, who can interpret these events? Who can explain events that have already taken place, and who can declare where they are leading?

> Present your case, Yahweh says.
> Produce your arguments, says the King of Jacob.
> Let them produce them and tell us what is going to happen.
> Tell us about the nature of previous events,
> so that we may give them our attention,
> and that we may know their outcome;
> or inform us of things to come.
> Tell us what is to come about in the future,
> so that we may know that you are gods.
> Do something, good or ill,
> so that we can look at it and see.
> It is clear, you and all you do are nothing at all.
> The person who chooses you is as disgusting as you are.
> I roused a man from the north, and he came.
> I roused one from the east, to call on my name.
> He has trampled on rulers as if they were clay,
> as if he was a potter treading it.
> Who announced this from the beginning, so that we could
>   know?
> Who announced it beforehand, so that we could say he was
>   right?
> There was no-one who announced it, no-one declared it.
> No-one heard you announce anything.
> I appoint an advocate for Zion,
> I give a herald for Jerusalem.
> But I looked, and there was no-one,

The faithful servant

> among them there was no counselor
> to give an answer when I ask a question.
> It is clear that they are idols,
> their deeds are nothing,
> their images are empty breath (41:21-29).

Yahweh, the God of Israel, is the one who long ago declared that Babylon would defeat Israel and that the Medes would defeat Babylon. Yahweh has thus shown the ability to decide to do something, and then do it. Earlier things have clearly come about; therefore the servant can be encouraged to believe the fresh things (42:9). The servant goes into God's world by God's summons, which arises from God's concern to be properly honored and is backed up by the proven power of God's word.

To whom does the servant calling apply?

Christians know that Jesus is the servant *par excellence*. But we have begun studying Isaiah 42 without referring to Jesus, listening to it as if we were the exiles when they heard the prophet's message for the first time. The exiles have been reminded that Israel is God's servant, and that this means God is committed to them (41:8-10). Now they are further reminded that to be God's servant means that they must be committed to God.

The story of Israel is the story of how God tried, and failed, to bring that about. His purpose was through Israel to reach the world. But the plan did not work. In an essay on "Prophecy and Fulfillment" (in a symposium called *Essays on Old Testament Interpretation* in Britain and *Essays on Old Testament Hermeneutics* in the USA, edited by C. Westermann), Rudolf Bultmann talks about the Old Testament as a whole as the story of the miscarriage of God's plan, the story of God's failure. That was why Jesus had to come, to succeed where Israel failed, so that (in a sense) God could succeed, having failed before. It is in this sense that Jesus is the servant, par excellence.

It is Jesus, then, who is the light of the world, who brings a covenant relationship with his father that everyone can enjoy. It is he who refuses to snap a broken reed or snuff out a flickering flame: we can see that in his personal caring for people like the failure Peter or the bereaved widow at Nain or the social outcast Zacchaeus or Mary Magdalene. It is he who is never dragged down by the weaknesses of these people who become his friends; he remains a burning and a shining light, he does not waver like a flickering candle. He also retains an unshakable confidence that God will bring his work to fruition, despite being let down by his people, his family, his friends, and his betrayer.

Yet Jesus' fulfillment of the servant's calling is not the end of its significance. The servant's task was to bring light to the nations, and Jesus was "the light to lighten the gentiles." But as well as saying of himself, "I am the light of the world" (John 8:12), he says to his followers, "You are the light of the world" (Matt. 5:14). "As the Father sent me, so I send you" (John 20:21). He returns the servant calling to the people of God to whom it first belonged.

These themes are ones to which we will return as we look at subsequent servant passages in Isaiah 40–55. But we can begin to note now that the servant calling needs to be looked at from the perspective of these three audiences. First it is a description of the calling of Israel, and in a sense it still is. But it is a calling mere human beings could not fulfill, indeed it depresses us, because it becomes a description of God's expectations that condemn us for our failure to live up to them (as the Torah became for Paul). So it becomes a description of the calling of Jesus, which he did live up to. But then it is also a description of the calling of the messianic people, and those who reckon to be members of the messianic people cannot escape its challenge to them.

CHAPTER EIGHT

The blind servant
Isaiah 42:18-48:22

In the course of describing the servant's position as the one to whom God is committed, and describing the servant's calling to be committed to God's purpose in the world, the Isaiah of the exile has given several hints that actually the Judean community cannot fulfill the servant's task. There is a tension between the two portraits. For instance, a key aspect of the task is that the servant should be the means of putting God's sovereignty into effect, of seeing that God's gracious and wise ordering of the world's affairs is a reality among the nations. But the prophet has referred earlier to God's sovereignty in relation to the people, and there the words concerned Jacob-Israel's complaint that Yahweh's sovereignty over its destiny was not apparent. We have mentioned already this expression of how it felt in exile: *the path I tread is hidden from Yahweh. My cause has passed out of God's notice* (40:27: the word for "cause" is the same as the one translated "government" in 42:1,3,4). The servant's task is to be concerned for the establishing of God's sovereign will in the world. But Israel is so worried about God's sovereign will for itself (naturally enough in the situation) that it seems unlikely to have the personal resources and energy to give itself in concern for God's sovereign purpose for other peoples. Yet that was the servant's task.

Again, the servant is not to *cry out or lift up his voice, or make it heard in the street.* But this is just what Jacob-Israel is doing when it laments Yahweh's having abandoned it. The servant will be someone who brings strength to broken reeds and who fans flickering flames, and someone who does not flicker or break himself. But the community in exile is a broken reed, a flickering flame. The servant is to bring sight to the blind and freedom to the prisoners; but Jacob-Israel is in bondage, and there are questions that might be asked about its spiritual sight.

So far the prophet's words have only hinted at this problem. They have said that Jacob-Israel is God's servant, and this is a comfort to it. They have then painted such a picture of what the servant will do that they simply leave one wondering very seriously whether the community can fulfill it. Eventually the point becomes explicit.

> You deaf people, listen!
> You blind, look and see! (42:18)

If the hearers have not picked up those hints, then they will naturally assume the prophet is speaking to the nations who are spiritually deaf and blind. But if the hearers thought that, they are now rudely awakened.

> Who is blind but my servant?
> Who is as deaf as the messenger I send?
> Who is as blind as my envoy?
> Who is as blind as Yahweh's servant?
> You see much, but you do not pay heed to it.
> He opens his ears, but he does not listen (42:19-20).

The point is now quite explicit. Jacob-Israel has the status of the servant, but not the spiritual sight and hearing necessary to someone who is to be God's messenger. It has sight, but not insight. It has heard all about Cyrus, and can put two and two

The blind servant

together and see the turmoil he is going to cause shortly in Babylon, but it cannot perceive that this is Yahweh's way of acting. So Yahweh cannot fulfill *his* purpose through it.

> Yahweh wanted, for the sake of his righteous purpose,
> to exalt the teaching and glorify it (42:21).

The prophet summarizes the purpose of God that the servant had been commissioned to fulfill, a purpose of righteousness in revealing the teaching for which the nations were looking (42:4,6). But God cannot achieve this through Israel. Here is the people that is supposed to embody the splendor of God's revelation and thus to prove it to the nations:

> But this is a people despoiled and plundered,
> trapped in holes, all of them,
> hidden in dungeons.
> They have become spoil with no-one to rescue it,
> plunder with no-one to say "Give it back" (42:22).

Further, they lack the insight to see the explanation for their predicament (42:23). In their prayers, it seems, they lamented the fact that they were given over to be pillaged and looted, and no doubt went on (as the Psalms do) to ascribe the responsibility for it to Yahweh. Indeed, they were right. It was Yahweh who had allowed it to happen. But they could not see the clear reason why Yahweh had done so.

> Who gave Jacob to the plunderer and Israel to the despoiler?
> Was it not Yahweh against whom we sinned,
>   in whose ways we were not willing to walk,
>   whose instruction we did not obey?
> So he poured on him the blaze of his anger and the fury of war
> (42:24-25).

Yahweh wanted to make a revelation to the world. The way of doing that was to show how well it worked in Israel. But in fact it did not work at all in Israel because Israel would not take it seriously. That is the explanation of why Jerusalem was destroyed and why Jacob-Israel was taken into exile, though it remains an explanation the exiles find difficult to accept.

> It wrapped him in flames, but he did not acknowledge this.
> It burned him, but he did not take it to heart (42:25).

They still cannot see it.

Of course this community was no more blind or deaf than average. They were behaving in the way that ordinary human beings do. The servant is only typically human. Paul makes that assumption himself when he talks about Israel and the church (Rom. 11). Israel is like an olive tree. When gentiles come to believe in the Messiah, they are like new branches grafted into that olive tree. There is room for so many of them to be grafted in because, fortunately for them, many of the original branches have been pruned out. But, Paul argues, it would be very dangerous if these new branches started to think that they were superior to the ones pruned out. They ought rather to learn humbly from them. Otherwise they risk the same fate themselves.

In the West, we ourselves live in an age in which the church often seems blind and in bondage. Compared with days in which it flourished, it is a pathetic minority in a world that totally ignores it. It has little influence on the life of the nations, and little reputation. Even when people start taking an interest in Jesus, it does not necessarily lead them to take an interest in us, the church. Furthermore, the church often seems to delight in hiding from the realities of the situation, in pretending that things are not so bad. Or it acknowledges that things are bad and sees this as the result of the world's opposition and sin. Yahweh reminded Jacob-Israel that its exile was not the result merely of the world's resistance to the truth or of Yahweh's own sleepiness. It was the result of their sin. The state of the church is not to be explained merely in economic or social terms. It raises questions about our attitude to God, as was the case with Israel.

So the servant who was supposed to bring sight to the blind and freedom to the prisoner is, by his own neglect, sightless and

The blind servant

in bondage. The natural step for God is therefore to retire him. In three ways, however, God says "No" to this possibility. "No," because I still love him (43:1-7). "No, because I still intend him to be my servant" (43:8-13). "No," because I am going to restore him (43:14-21 and following sections).

"No," because I still love him

We have already learned something of God's attitude to people who are blind and imprisoned or broken and wavering. God has declared a concern to bring them sight and freedom, strength and renewal (42:1-9). He was talking there about those to whom Israel was supposed to minister. But if Israel itself comes to have needs like that, then perhaps it can receive the ministry that people like that need? This is actually one of the moving aspects of these chapters. Often the prophet speaks about the needy without specifying who the needy are. God's ideal was that Israel should be the strong one, with the resources to bring strength to the weak. But the fact that the prophet does not keep saying, "I mean Israel here," "I mean the gentiles here," enables the words to be applied as they need to be, to whoever the strong and the weak are. If Israel is needy, it can *receive* the ministry it is supposed to give.

In practice, the people of God (and those who are particularly called to minister within the people of God, or to embody its mission to those outside) live with an alternation between these two pictures of themselves. Their model of ministry or mission has commonly been the hero or heroine whose relationship with God never falters, whose commitment never hesitates, whose love never runs out, whose patience never tires. Their ministry to the weak, the needy, and the doubting therefore never flags. That model can lead to the belief that those who minister can never themselves show weakness or need (and must therefore hide it from themselves and from others), and this belief has in turn led sometimes to the entire rejection of the model, as being unreal. That is an over-reaction. Those who minister *are* called to embody that model. But they remain human and frail, and have weaknesses and needs, which cannot (and need not) be finally denied or hidden. The grace of God, which in moments of strength can be applied to others, in moments of need can be applied to oneself. If we cannot be Yahweh's servant dispensing Yahweh's strength to the weak, we can be Yahweh's servant receiving Yahweh's strength for the weak.

Yet one of the consequences of becoming for a time broken and wavering oneself, and in need of being ministered to because one is no longer in a state to minister, is that one is no longer capable of applying the promises and the grace of God to oneself (let alone to others). This was certainly the situation of the exiles. The prophet brings them no new message, but merely reminds them of old truths about God as their creator, their sovereign, and their "guardian," old truths that are embodied in the story of their history and in the praise of their psalms. They are quite familiar with these; yet they have quite forgotten them. They are no longer able to take them into account. So the servant who is weak and unable to serve has to be ministered to. This perhaps implies that in a time of strength a servant has to be concerned not only to minister to the weak, but also to make sure of having ways to be ministered to when a time of weakness comes. In such circumstances we need people to whom we can go, or we need to know what parts of Scripture to direct ourselves to. There have to be ways in which the servant can receive ministry when in no state to minister.

Indeed, the prophet promises this to Yahweh's servant.

> But now this is the word of Yahweh,
> the one who created you, Jacob,
> the one who formed you, Israel:
> Do not be afraid, I have restored you.
> I called you by name. You belong to me.
> When you pass through the sea, I will be with you.
> When you pass through the rivers, they will not overwhelm you.

The blind servant

> When you walk through fire you will not be touched,
> the flame will not burn you.
> Because I, Yahweh, am your God,
> I, the holy one of Israel, am your deliverer,
> I give Egypt as your ransom,
> Sudan and Ethiopia in return for you.
> Because you are precious in my eyes,
> because of the honor you have and because I love you,
> I give human beings in return for you,
> I give peoples in return for your life.
> Do not be afraid, I am with you.
> I will bring your descendants from the east,
> I will gather you from the west,
> I will say to the north, "Give them up,"
> and to the south, "Do not hold them back."
> "Bring my sons from far away,
> bring my daughters from the end of the earth,
> each one of those who call themselves by my name,
> whom I created, whom I formed,
> whom I made, for my glory" (43:1-7).

The prophet reiterates previous declarations about Yahweh's purpose to restore Israel (compare especially 41:8-20). The words begin and end with the assertion that it was Yahweh who created Israel in the first place, to be Yahweh's in a special sense (43:1,7). That is a further reason for their believing that Yahweh really will look after them and bring them back. Burning and captivity (42:22,24,25) are not Yahweh's last word to them (43:2,5-6). Yahweh would give anything for them (43:3b-4). And at the base of these promises and these declarations is fundamentally a relationship between God and them and an attitude on God's part that values and honors and loves them (43:2-3a).

Some of these expressions are new, but even where the words are the same as they have been earlier, it is not mere repetition, for the previous paragraph that spoke of Israel's blindness and deafness (42:18-25) was an accusation. The words and the style would be familiar to the prophet's hearers from everyday life. The accused has no scope for self-defense in face of this accusation. There is no doubt that the elders gathered at the city gate would declare that the case was proven. So all there is to follow is the sentencing. Israel has rebelled against Yahweh and failed to show the slightest insight even when it has been chastised. Therefore....

But this is not what follows. The prophet's next word (43:1) is not "therefore"; it is "but." "But" is one of the important recurrent introductions to the grace and the power of God as the Bible speaks of it. What is quite unexpected, humanly speaking, comes about by God's power (for instance, Acts 2:24), God's mercy (Eph. 2:24), or God's providence (Gen. 50:20). So it is here. The sentence that one expects will follow incontrovertible guilt is not passed. Instead Yahweh's commitment to the people is reasserted. "You are still the one I chose and called by name, the one I love. I am with you." These declarations are reiterated after God and the people have together looked further into the depth of the people's blindness, deafness, and uselessness. God hides from none of the truth about Israel. Indeed God brings it all out into the open, and then declares, "But I still love you."

If that was the word of God to the exiles in the sixth century BC, it has at least two sets of implications for the twenty-first century AD. It has implications for the actual descendants of Old Testament Israel, for the Jewish people. The Isaiah of the exile declared that God was committed to Israel no matter what happened, despite their sin. This is often not how the Christian church has looked at the Jewish people. A terrible toll of Christian persecution of Jewish people has been exacted over the past two millennia and remains on the conscience of the church of Christ. The church has seen the Jews as the crucifiers of Jesus, but not as the people of God to whom God is irrevocably committed.

That commitment is not only an Old Testament belief. Paul believes that the Jews in his day are the objects of God's wrath, because they have rejected and killed the Messiah and try to

The blind servant

stifle the messianic gospel (1 Thes. 1:16). Like Isaiah of the exile, he speaks as a Jew to Jews, and his understanding of the position of the Jews is similar to that of the prophet. But also like the prophet, Paul declares that nevertheless God is still committed to Israel, even though it refuses to commit itself to the Messiah—because "the gifts and the call of God are irrevocable" (Rom. 11:29). That phrase could be a summary of the gospel according to Isaiah in the exile: all Paul does in his theological discussion of the place of the Jews is restate that message in the light of the shock of the Jews' rejection of Jesus. That will not be the end, Paul says; God is still committed to Israel, so the time will come when they find salvation. For God still loves them. They may not escape the fire and the flood unharmed (as the exiles were promised they would, 43:2); but God still goes with them through the fire and the flood, and even brings new birth out of holocaust. Still he says to them, *You belong to me* (43:1).

That relationship and the promises that issue from it remain real for the actual descendants of the exiles. They are given new extent and depth in the gospel of Christ for all who believe in him, both Jew and Gentile. In John's Gospel, Jesus makes this point by describing himself as the good shepherd, caring not only for his accustomed (Jewish) flock, but also for other sheep beyond that. They are secure with him; no-one can snatch them from his hand, still less from the hand of his Father (John 10:14, 16,28,29).

That image takes us back to Isaiah, for here Yahweh returning to Jerusalem is pictured not only as a victorious warrior, but also as a caring shepherd:

> Like a shepherd he tends his flock,
> he gathers the lambs with his arm,
> he carries them in his arms,
> he leads the ewes to water (40:11).

And no-one is able to snatch them out of the Father's hand. No matter how unworthy we may seem, no matter how unworthy we may really become, God says to us all, "You are still the one I chose, the one I called by name, the one I love. Do not be afraid, I am with you." And even when God and we have together looked at our blindness and deafness and uselessness, God still declares, "But I love you all the same."

"No," because I still intend to use him as my servant

The blind and deaf servant is not to be cast off, not only because God still loves him, but also because God has not abandoned the plan to use him. In the reiteration of Israel's relationship with God at which we have been looking, one note is conspicuous by its absence. *Fear not, I am with you, I have redeemed you, I am your God....* But one crucial description of Jacob-Israel is missing. It is not described as God's servant.

It would perhaps have been a quite understandable compromise on God's part. The commitment to Israel would still stand—it would still be God's people, it would be restored, delivered, kept in God's arms of love. But God would realistically acknowledge that it did not really seem possible to use Israel as the servant by means of which to fulfill the purpose of reaching out to the world. It would not be sacked, but it would be kicked upstairs.

That possibility is now ruled out by what follows.

> Bring out the people that are blind, though they have eyes,
> that are deaf, though they have ears.
> All the nations have gathered together,
> the peoples have assembled.
> Who among them could have announced this,
> could have told us of the events that are now past?
> Let them produce their witnesses to prove them right,
> so that people may hear and say, "It is true."
> You are my witnesses, Yahweh says,
> you are my servant whom I chose,
> so that you may know and trust in me,
> so that you might see that I am the one.

The blind servant

> Before me no god was formed,
> and after me there will be none.
> It is I, I am Yahweh, and there is no deliverer apart from me.
> It was I who announced it, I delivered you,
> I declared it, and there was no stranger among you.
> And you are my witnesses, Yahweh says.
> I am God; in the future too, I am the one.
> There is no-one who can take things from my hand.
> I act, and who can reverse it? (43:8-13).

The servant is deaf and the witnesses are blind, but Yahweh still wants witnesses, in order to have someone to testify regarding who alone is sovereign in history, and Yahweh still intends that Israel should act as these witnesses, as this servant. Indeed, the prophet says, Yahweh is telling them that they are still to act as God's servant because this in itself will lead to the building up of their faith.

It is possible that the prophet has in mind here the striking fact that having to function as God's witness builds up faith in God. This is certainly true in experience. But more likely he means something slightly different. It is rather that actually telling Israel that it is still God's servant, still God's witnesses, is a means of building up its faith in God, because it is difficult to imagine how God could say anything that was more gracious, more loving, and more calculated to win its love and response. God says to it, "I know you are blind, I know you are deaf, I know you are in prison. I know you are finding it more and more difficult to believe in me, and to believe that I care about you. So how can I encourage your faith, how can I win your response? Can I do it by telling you this? If I am to reveal myself to the world I need someone to be my servant, my witnesses. That is the most important role I could give to anyone. And I am giving it to you. Now do you believe that I am committed to you?"

Again, if those were God's words to the exiles in the sixth century BC, they are suggestive with regard to the position of both the Jewish people and the Christian church nearly three millennia later. God's commitment to Israel, God's irrevocable gifts and calling, consist not merely in Israel's still being God's chosen one. They mean God still intends to use Israel as a servant and as witnesses. Paul also takes up this aspect of God's commitment to Israel. He not only asserts that Israel is going to be saved. He also declares that Israel is again to be a means of blessing to the world. It is because of Israel's rejection of the Messiah that the church came to concentrate on bringing the good news of Jesus to the gentiles (see Acts 13:44-49). But "if their trespass means riches for the world, and if their failure means riches for the Gentiles, how much more will their full inclusion mean.... If their rejection means the reconciliation of the world, what will their acceptance mean but life from the dead?" (Rom. 11:12, 15 RSV). The words are vague; Paul is not precise in the way he speaks. But he implies that there is a further role for God's servant Israel yet to fulfill as a witness in the world.

But the Gentile-Jewish Christian church also inherits God's promises. To them, too, God denies going back on making people servants. We can go back on our commitment to God. We can slide gradually away and commit acts that are quite unworthy of God. We can seem to ourselves unforgivable and unrestorable, as those who have gone too far away and have sullied ourselves too much. But to disobedient, faithless, hopeless people God still says, *You are my witnesses... you are my servant... so that you may know and trust in me* (43:10). Paradoxically, of course, in a sense we will be able to prove God's grace even more convincingly than we could before, because we demonstrate that God's love for people is totally and solely dependent on God and not at all on people's qualifications. Thus, however far away from God we may drift, we are never disqualified from being God's servants or God's witnesses, because the reason for our being God's witnesses never did lie in our qualifications. It lay in God's choice, and that choice stands. God still says, *You are my witnesses.*

The blind servant

"No," because I am going to restore him

Isaiah of the exile goes on to add (and to develop at some length) a further response to the question whether the imprisoned and blind servant is to be cast off. Those experiences of imprisonment and blindness suggest two different problems that the prophet (and Yahweh) have to face. The one is more outward and material, the other more inward and spiritual. So far many of the prophecies have been quite general, even vague. We have assumed that the warrior from the east is Cyrus, that his people are the Persians, that it is the Babylonians that they threaten, and so on, but none of these parties has been actually named. Now the picture starts to come into focus as the prophet declares how the exiles' outward, material, political problem will be dealt with.

> These are the words of Yahweh,
> your redeemer, the holy one of Israel:
> For your sake I have sent to Babylon,
> and I will lay them prostrate as fugitives, all of them,
> the Chaldeans in the ships they exult in (43:14).

The agent of this act, King Cyrus himself, is soon named in turn for the first time.

> Thus says Yahweh, your redeemer,
> he who formed you in the womb:
> I, myself, Yahweh, made all things....
> I am he who says of Cyrus, "My shepherd—
> he will fulfill my whole purpose,
> saying of Jerusalem, "Let it be rebuilt,"
> and of the Temple, "Let your foundation be laid"
> Thus says Yahweh to his anointed, to Cyrus,
> whom he has taken by his right hand
> to subdue nations before him
> and strip the loins of kings,
> to force gateways before him
> that their gates be closed no more:

> I will go before you leveling the heights.
> I will shatter the bronze gateways,
> smash the iron bars.
> I will give you the hidden treasures,
> the secret hoards,
> that you may know that I am Yahweh,
> the God of Israel, who calls you by your name (44:24, 28; 45:1-3 JB).

Cyrus is Yahweh's anointed (45:1). That is a rather extraordinary statement. The Hebrew word for "anointed" is "messiah." In the time before the exile, the "anointed one," the messiah, is the king of David's line. When there is no king of David's line, the messiah is the Davidic king that people hope will occupy that throne in the future. But the Isaiah of the exile is so convinced that Cyrus is (unknown to himself) Yahweh's agent that he sees him as the fulfillment of the promises concerning the messiah.

It was Cyrus, too, who would expose the impotence of the Babylonian gods. They are in turn now named for the first time.

> Bel has crouched down, Nebo has stooped low:
> their images, once carried in your processions,
> have been loaded on to beasts and cattle,
> a burden for the weary creatures;
> they stoop and they crouch;
> not for them to bring the burden to safety;
> the gods themselves go into captivity (46:1-2 NEB).

The gods that were formerly carried in procession are carried to safety when the city's downfall is imminent (actually their priests stayed in Babylon and changed sides when Cyrus arrived, but perhaps that act makes their gods' impotence even clearer). The prophet enjoys bringing out the irony of the scene: "I thought that your gods were supposed to support you, not that you had to support your gods!" At least Yahweh can carry the exiles:

> Listen to me, house of Jacob
> and all the remnant of the house of Israel,

The blind servant

> a load on me from your birth, carried by me from the womb:
> till you grow old I am He,
> and when white hairs come, I will carry you still;
> I have made you and I will bear the burden,
> I will carry you and bring you to safety (46:3-4 NEB).

The prophet goes on to describe Babylon itself as a woman who was once so fine, so stately, so impressive, so proud, but is now humiliated and exiled as Israel had once been (see Isaiah 47). Thus, Israel can go free:

> Come out of Babylon! Run from the Chaldeans!
> Shout out the news, proclaim this message,
> send it out to the ends of the earth,
> say, Yahweh has redeemed his servant Jacob! (48:20).

The Isaiah of the exile thus offers Jacob-Israel encouragement after encouragement about the physical restoration of the people. Cyrus will arrive, Babylon will be defeated, the exiles will return home, Jerusalem will be restored. The exiles are in bondage, in prison. But they are to be released.

At the same time as one reads these repeated promises of restoration, however, one notices another contrasting aspect of the people's need emerging. From the beginning of these prophecies, it is true, they have been described as demoralized, their faith exhausted, their hope gone, their spirit unable to comprehend what Yahweh is doing with them. They were very needy, though not actively rebellious. But as these promises unfold, and the message of restoration is expounded, a surprising feature emerges. Israel seems to be resisting God's word. It now seems to be rebellious.

This is hinted at in the urgent way the prophet has to repeat statements. We have noted the declaration that Israel could not really be God's servant because of its sin, but that nevertheless God is still committed to it, still wants it as his witnesses, and still plans to restore it (42:18–43:21). When that comes to an end, it is repeated, point by point, with perhaps greater emphasis (43:22–45:8). In the light of what follows, the reason for this seems to be that the prophet found the exiles would not listen to the message. It had to be repeated and re-emphasized.

The exiles are not merely reluctant to listen; they are actively resistant to the message. The prophet declared that Yahweh was going to use Cyrus to restore Judah. He was Yahweh's anointed. It seems that in some quarters this was a very unwelcome message. It was almost as if someone in modern Israel began to talk about the President of the USA as the Messiah. So the prophet has to deal with those who resist the message.

> Does a clay pot dare to argue with its maker,
> a pot that is like all the others?
> Does the clay ask the potter what he is doing?
> Does the pot complain that its maker has no skill?
> Does anyone dare to say to his parents,
> "Why did you make me like this?"
> The LORD, the holy God of Israel,
> the one who shapes the future, says:
> "You have no right to question me about my children
> or tell me what I ought to do!
> I am the one who made the earth
> and created mankind to live there.
> By my power I stretched out the heavens;
> I control the sun, the moon, and the stars.
> I myself have stirred Cyrus to action
> to fulfill my purpose and put things right.
> I will straighten every road that he travels.
> He will rebuild my city, Jerusalem,
> and set my captive people free.
> No one has hired him or bribed him to do this.
> The LORD Almighty has spoken (45:9-13 GNB).

The message about the exposure of the Babylonian gods also leads in to a challenge to those who oppose his message.

> Remember this and take it to heart.
> Recall it to mind, you rebels....

> Listen to me, you stubborn-hearted,
> you who are so far away from my righteous purpose.
> I have brought my righteous purpose near, it is not far away…
> (46:8,12,13).

The point comes out most clearly after the chapter that describes the humiliation of Babylon itself.

> Listen to this, people of Israel,
> you that are descended from Judah:
> You swear by the name of the LORD
> and claim to worship the God of Israel—
> but you don't mean a word you say.
> And yet you are proud to say
> that you are citizens of the holy city
> and that you depend on Israel's God,
> whose name is the LORD Almighty.
> The LORD says to Israel,
> "Long ago I predicted what would take place;
> then suddenly I made it happen.
> I knew that you would prove to be stubborn,
> as rigid as iron and unyielding as bronze.
> And so I predicted your future long ago,
> announcing events before they took place,
> to prevent you from claiming
> that your idols and images made them happen.
> All I foretold has now taken place;
> you have to admit my predictions were right.
> Now I will tell you of new things to come,
> events that I did not reveal before.
> Only now am I making them happen;
> nothing like this took place in the past.
> If it had, you would claim that you knew all about it.
> I knew that you couldn't be trusted,
> that you have always been known as a rebel.
> That is why you never heard of this at all,
> why no word of it ever came to your ears.
> In order that people will praise my name,

God's Prophet, God's Servant

> I am holding my anger in check;
> I am keeping it back and will not destroy you.
> I have tested you in the fire of suffering,
> as silver is refined in a furnace.
> But I have found that you are worthless.
> If only you had listened to my commands!
> Then blessings would have flowed for you
> like a stream that never goes dry!
> Victory would have come to you
> like the waves that roll on the shore.
> Your descendants would be as numerous as grains of sand,
> and I would have made sure they were never destroyed...
> "There is no safety for sinners," says the LORD
> (48:1-10, 18-20, 22 GNB).

So the prophet makes it more and more explicit and clear how Israel is to be restored nationally and politically through Cyrus, but also makes Israel's inner problem more and more clear. Through the prophet's being sent to tell the exiles how their material needs were to be met, there comes to the surface the exiles' loss of faith, their inability to learn, their slowness to turn to God, their resistance to God's will, the unreality of their profession of response to God, their spiritual obstinacy, their cynicism, their inclination to place their trust anywhere but in God.

There is no "shalom" for rebels (48:22). In the church today, there is much talk of *shalom*, that wholeness in all aspects of human life that is God's purpose for us. *Shalom* includes both the material and the spiritual, and it is easy for one or other of these to become all-important. The witness of Isaiah 40–55 is that God cares about the people's outward welfare, but that it is possible to be restored to one's land and to have a new Jerusalem and a new temple, without having a new heart. If the people of God find outward success but no inward renewal, they do not find real *shalom*. Cyrus is to bring the exiles back to Judah, but who will bring them back to God? Before Israel can function as God's servant, it needs someone to fulfill a servant ministry to it. So who is to be a servant for Israel?

CHAPTER NINE

The persistent servant
Isaiah 49-50

So Isaiah 40–48 reveals Yahweh's plan for bringing the people back to their homeland, and declares that the plan is in process of fulfillment. But it also raises more and more sharply the question how Israel is to be brought back to God. How can it find the real shalom that is impossible for rebels against God? It is this task that we are now told is to be fulfilled by Yahweh's servant. Yahweh *formed me in the womb to be his servant, to bring Jacob back to him, so that Israel might be gathered to him* (49:5). It is the calling of Yahweh's servant to bring Israel back to Yahweh.

Now we have noted that scholars have puzzled endlessly over who the prophet means by the servant in Isaiah 40–55. Sometimes it is explicit that Israel is the servant (for instance, 41:8-10 and 44:1-2), and I have suggested that elsewhere, too, in the chapters we have looked at, the natural view is that Israel is meant to be the servant (notably 42:1-9). The servant is supposed to be Israel; yet this servant is blind and imprisoned (42:18-25). It cannot fulfill the servant's task and someone has to be a servant to Israel. The problem about understanding who

God's Prophet, God's Servant

Second Isaiah means by the servant arises out of that complication: Israel is the servant, but Israel needs a servant to minister to it, as the prophet now makes explicit.

So who is this servant who is to minister to Israel?

> Listen to me, coastlands!
> Pay heed, distant peoples!
> Yahweh called me before I was born.
> When I was still in my mother's womb he named my name.
> He made my mouth like a sharp sword
> and hid me in his hand.
> He made me a polished arrow
> and concealed me in his quiver.
> He said to me, "You are my servant..." (49:1-3).

Words like those are familiar enough from the testimonies of prophets. These particular words are especially reminiscent of Jeremiah's account of how Yahweh called him to be a prophet: how he formed him for this purpose from the womb and put his words in Jeremiah's mouth (Jer. 1:5,9). It is a prophet who is speaking here. This is the calling and ministry of the Isaiah of the exile.

For this prophet has indeed been seeking to minister to Israel, and seeking to understand what God is doing with it, and to perceive what are its needs. Second Isaiah has seen more and more clearly that it does need someone to minister to it before it can minister to others, and has perhaps wondered, "*How* is Yahweh going to meet these inner needs of Israel so that it can serve Yahweh again? How is Yahweh going to bring Israel back to God?" Perhaps it was now like a shattering realization dawning. "I am the one Yahweh intends to use." Of course it is often the case that the person who perceives a need and comes to be burdened about something is the person God is going to use to meet that need. There is a certain risk involved in becoming too interested in and concerned in this way: it can turn out to be part of God's preparation of a servant.

So here in 49:1-6 we are being given a description of the

calling and ministry of the one whom God purposes to use as servant to the servant, the one who will minister to the deepest needs of the people of God in exile. Shortly, in 50:4-9, we are given a further testimony relating to the experience of seeking to fulfill this calling. Together, these two passages suggest various insights on what it means to be Yahweh's servant.

He is one who is prepared by God

Yahweh called me before I was born. When I was still in my mother's womb he named my name (49:1). We have already considered Jeremiah's account of his call, where the words are similar. Yahweh's involvement goes back to the very beginning—to the prophet's very formation as a person. Yahweh had a role in mind for this person even then. From the beginning Yahweh was preparing the prophet for it.

The implication is that God had even allowed for the ways plans would need to be modified in the light of the interplay between God's own purpose and the attitudes of those God seeks to use. We ourselves are used to the experience of things not turning out as we planned; we do our best to anticipate what may go wrong with our schemes, but we accept that unforeseen obstacles are nevertheless bound to arise. We shall need to revise our plans and adapt them as we are implementing them. In one sense God himself also does that: the prophet's calling to be the servant arises from the revision of God's plan in the light of the exiles' resistance to the message. But God can anticipate the obstacles that imperil plans and can allow for their revision even before they are implemented. So the prophet's call to be the servant is not a hasty botching of an imperfect scheme. It had been allowed for and the prophet had been prepared for it even before the snag had actually manifested itself. So when unexpected things happen to God's servants or they have to be drafted in to fill sudden gaps, they may still be involved in the outworking of what God had allowed for long ago. Further, if God takes account from the beginning of how different servants can be used in particular situations, then this implies the capacity to take account of each event and experience in their lives as these unfold. No "accidents" happen to them. All that they experience is taken account of by the God who knows about it before they are born.

So God prepared this servant for a specific task. *He made my mouth like a sharp sword and hid me in his hand. He made me a polished arrow and concealed me in his quiver* (49:2). From the very beginning the prophet was prepared, like a sword made ready in its sheath, or like an arrow in its quiver waiting to be used. The comparison with a sword or an arrow suggests a ministry that was not to be confined to bringing a message of comfort (despite 40:1). Or perhaps the prophet now recognizes for the first time that the message has to be confrontational in order to bring real comfort. Second Isaiah is in the midst of experiencing resistance to the message, even though it is a message of good news. The people resist the message for various reasons: they did not like the way God proposed to go about restoring them, they found the message too good to be true, they discovered that they had to face up to some uncomfortable truths about themselves. Despite the message of comfort, the Isaiah of the exile had to be confrontational. The message brought not peace, but a sword. But the prophet was aware of having been prepared for that. As a servant of God, he was one with whom God had been involved from birth as the Lord of the events and experiences of the life that unfolded even before God's summons. All these had played their part in connection with the particular task God now had in mind.

As we noted in the case of Jeremiah, this could seem like a tyranny: "I am not free to make my own decisions, I am merely a cog in a wheel." But for the Isaiah of the exile it is, on the contrary, a valuable reassurance when under pressure. The prophet took on a ministerial role among the exiles that brought personal cost and seemed rather unsuccessful. But it was all within the providence and purpose of a loving God who does not make mistakes. Yahweh planned this role. The prophet is in the right place.

The servant is one who will live up to what it means to be Israel

> He said to me, "You are my servant,
> you are Israel in whom I shall take pride" (49:3).

Here are three descriptions of the prophet. *"You are my servant."* There is nothing very surprising about a prophet being described in this way. In the Old Testament, kings and prophets are regularly described as God's servant, and Isaiah of Jerusalem spoke of himself in these terms (Isa. 20:3). On the other hand, all that has been said about the calling of God's servant so far in these chapters adds to the dimensions of what God now means when he says to the prophet, "You are my servant."

Even so, we are not prepared for the surprise of what then follows. "You are my servant, you are Israel." Some scholars have found it so surprising that the prophet should identify himself with Israel that they have concluded that this must be a mistake that crept in as the scribes went about their task of copying down the text of the book of Isaiah. But that is rather too easy a way to dispose of a surprising statement. We ought to try to make sense of it as it stands. It surely reflects the prophet's discovery that Israel in exile is not really capable at the moment of living up to what it means to be Israel. To be Israel is to be God's own possession, a kingdom of priests and a holy nation (Exod. 19:5-6). It is to be a people who love, trust, obey, serve, and fear the living God. It is to be a people open to God's blessing and keen to reflect God to the world. But Israel as a whole cannot be those things at the moment. The outward Israel does not have the real Israel's characteristics.

This is not a new situation. It happened, for instance, in the time of Elijah and in the time of Jeremiah. At moments like that, only individuals such as those prophets seem to behave like Israel. The Isaiah of the exile is one of that line. This prophet alone gives God the response that the real Israel gives. Second Isaiah is the real Israel. *You are my servant, you are Israel...*

… in whom I shall take pride. Israel was supposed to be the body in whom Yahweh took pride (44:23). The prophet uses a word that refers, for instance, to a woman's finery. God wants to parade Israel before the world and before the other so-called gods, and say, as it were, "Are you not impressed by this achievement of mine?" The way Israel has behaved has made that impossible. But God's desire is nearer to fulfillment in the prophet's own life. Second Isaiah has opened up to receiving insight into Yahweh's purpose and has sought to serve Yahweh. The prophet is willing to be one of whom Yahweh can be proud.

When Paul expresses for himself the conviction held by Jeremiah and by Second Isaiah that God had set him apart for his service even before he was born, he goes on to describe his actual conversion and calling as the revealing of God's Son in him (Gal. 1:15-16). It was not merely a revelation *to* Paul, but something that came to be embodied *in* his life, so that from then on God was revealed *through* him. Isaiah of the exile, too, is to be the means of God's message reaching other people. But this comes about in part through being the embodiment of what Israel is itself called to be. The prophet is the servant Israel in whom God can take pride; embodying this vocation is a means to ministering to Israel as it is, so that it can be restored to this calling. God's servants are summoned to embody what it means to be God's people, to incarnate what they are calling God's people to. It is a solemn task. But John Calvin, in his comment on this verse, also notes that it should be an encouragement.

> This is a very high honour conferred on poor, feeble men, when the Lord appoints them, though corrupt and depraved, to promote his glory; and therefore we ought to be the more encouraged to render to him our service and obedience (*Commentary on the Book of the Prophet Isaiah*, Volume 4, p. 12).

The servant is someone who is called to embody what it means to be Israel; he will live up to that calling.

The servant is one in whom hope, in end, wins the victory over despair

> But I said, "I have worked to no purpose,
> I have spent my strength to achieve absolutely nothing" (49:4).

The prophet surveys the ministry we have been considering. What is there to show for it? What fruit is there? It seems, none. All Second Isaiah gets is looks of incredulity and words of disbelief. This whole ministry as the prophet reviews it seems to have been pointless, useless, futile. If Second Isaiah had never taken up this task, it would not have made the slightest difference to where the exiles were in relation to God. Like the exiles, the prophet is a broken reed, a wavering flame, one who has, after all, succumbed to the weaknesses of the people themselves.

That is what is threatened. But the prophet does not let this voice of despair have the last word. Related to the servant's own need for ministry is the importance of arguing with oneself when one is under pressure. As we saw in the case of Jeremiah, the doubts and agonies inside have to be expressed; it is not necessary or wise to bottle them up. But then they have to be examined critically. When inclined to think that this work is pointless and useless, God's servant has to stand back and ask what other factors need to be taken into account that one may be forgetting. This is necessary if the judgment is to be a balanced one.

The trouble with Israel was that when it was broken and fading it had failed to look at its situation from God's perspective. It had stopped taking God into account. It believed that Yahweh was no longer concerned about what was right for it (40:27). The prophet does not fall into that trap. Second Isaiah thinks about the personal application of the message delivered earlier. Yahweh does act in sovereignty and is concerned that people should see that sovereignty put into effect (42:1, 3, 4). So here the prophet declares,

> Yet my judgment is in Yahweh's hands,
> my reward is in God's hands (49:4).

My judgment is a word we have looked at earlier (40:27; 42:1, 3,4). Israel doubted if Yahweh was any longer concerned to implement a purpose for it, and therefore it was unable to be the means of Yahweh's revealing to the nations what God's sovereignty in their lives might look like. The prophet does not fall into this disbelief. Yahweh is in control.

How does Second Isaiah know? If we are to take account of the message delivered earlier, it is surely through looking at what Yahweh has said and done in the past. Yahweh has demonstrated faithfulness in the past and *will* honor this servant again. Second Isaiah is God's servant, and hope wins the victory over despair within this servant, in the end, because the afflictions of present experience are not allowed to erase from the mind the grounds for confidence in God that previous personal experience and knowledge of God's dealings with the people have given.

The servant is one with a task in relation to the people of God and in relation to the world

The prophet goes on to refer to three tasks that Isaiah 40–55 as a whole is concerned with.

> But now this is the word of Yahweh,
> who formed me in the womb to be his servant.
> to bring Jacob back to him,
> so that Israel might be gathered to him,
> so that I am honored in Yahweh's sight
> and my God is my strength (49:5).

The first task is to bring the people back to God, the task that remains unfulfilled when Cyrus brings it back to Judah. It is this calling that the prophet here tells us he realizes God gives him. He himself has been identified by the name Israel, because at present the empirical Israel, the Israel that can be seen, does not deserve the name. But the name still belongs to it, and the

The persistant servant

servant's task is to embody in his own life what it means to be Israel, but then to be involved in ministry to the Israel that can be seen, so that it can become the real Israel. It is this task that the prophet has been having his doubts about. He is not sure he is getting anywhere. He is having to argue with himself over whether Yahweh is really going to prosper his ministry. Now, if one were allowed to speak in the council of Yahweh, one might want to suggest that the prophet should be given some relief from this task if he cannot be given more support in it. But this is not Yahweh's reaction when the prophet says he is feeling the pressure. On the contrary, Yahweh increases the dimensions of what he expects Isaiah of the exile to achieve.

But first, Yahweh refers to the second of the tasks Isaiah 40–55 as a whole is concerned with, but that is not the business of his servant.

> He says, It is too slight a task for you to be my servant
> to re-establish the tribes of Jacob
> and bring back what has been preserved of Israel (49:6).

Re-establishing the tribes of Jacob and bringing back the preserved of Israel to their own land is what we have referred to as the material, political aspect to Israel's restoration. It is to be brought out of bondage and re-established in its own land, but that will all be achieved by means of Cyrus, the foreign king. It is really not at all the most important task there is to do. The Persians can and will achieve that. It is too slight and unimportant a task for God's servant.

The note the prophet strikes here sounds an unfashionable one. We have noted that often Christians have not shown enough interest and involvement in political matters, while at other times they have become over-preoccupied with these questions. It is difficult to get a balanced view of their importance. A balance involves neither under-emphasizing nor overemphasizing them. At the moment many Christians are placing considerable stress on them. The view of Isaiah of the exile is that they are important, but that they are the distinctive concern of the secular authorities, not that of the servant of Yahweh. To translate his view into Christian terms, he might hold that it was appropriate for Christians to be involved in politics and in government, as human beings concerned for the fair and efficient management of the world God created. But this involvement is not the task of the ministry or of the church as the church. That is too slight a task compared on the one hand with the challenge of being concerned for the relationship between God's people and God himself (verse 5) and on the other hand with the third task he now speaks of.

> I shall appoint you as a light to the nations
> so that my salvation may reach the ends of the earth (49:6).

One way in which this will come about is indirect. We have seen already that when Israel really becomes Israel, this is to have a shattering effect on the world. So if the prophet as Yahweh's servant exercises an effective ministry in bringing Israel back to God and enabling it really to function as Israel, then his ministry is going to affect the world, too, in an indirect way.

There is probably also a direct way in which it affects the world. Perhaps we are to imagine him preaching to the Babylonians themselves as well as to the exiles. Certainly he has brought light to many generations since, whatever he actually did in his lifetime. And certainly his words became part of the rationale for the first Christians' preaching to the gentiles. The New Testament includes only one direct quotation from these two first-person testimonies of the prophet as servant (49:1-6 and 50:4-9), and it refers the passage not to Jesus but to the ministry of the apostles. Paul and Barnabas were preaching in the synagogue and to gentile crowds in Antioch, in Turkey. The Jews are displeased at the impact they are having among the gentiles, but Paul justifies his turning to the gentiles by quoting this text: "For so the Lord commanded us, 'I have appointed you to be a light for the nations, so that you may bring salvation to the end of the earth'" (Acts 13:47). Paul finds the pattern for his Christian ministry in the prophet's description of his call.

The persistant servant

He, too, failed with the Jews, and the prophet's testimony suggests that he turns his attention to the gentiles. The servant is one with a task in relation to Israel and to the world.

The one who listens in order to be able to speak

After that first servant testimony, the chapters revert for a while to messages of reassurance to Israel and to accounts of how Israel (or rather Zion-Jerusalem personified) finds it so difficult to believe that Yahweh is still concerned for it (49:7-50:3). Then the testimony resumes (50:4-11). The first episode showed us how the prophet had been prepared for a ministry involving words that were sharp, penetrating, and confrontational. Here Yahweh commissions words that are less confrontational, more supportive.

> The Lord Yahweh has given me a disciple's tongue,
> so that I could know how to support the weary.
> With a word he arouses me in the morning,
> in the morning he arouses my hearing,
> so that I listen like a disciple (50:4).

It is easy for a person full of words to increase rather than relieve someone's weariness. This was true of Job's so-called comforters. They had been at their best when they sat silently with Job, almost in the manner of the family and friends of a Jew "sitting shiva" with someone in a time of bereavement. But when Job's friends opened their mouths, it was to add to rather than to alleviate his affliction. There is a time not to speak.

The art and ministry of listening has been rightly stressed in recent years in connection with counseling. But there is a time to speak. When we have come to understand the precise nature of someone's weariness, our privilege and responsibility is not only to show them that we share it, but also to apply the gospel to it. If we fail to add speaking to our listening, then our silence is guilty. To express sympathy and say how sorry you are may be useless. But that does not mean there are no words to say.

Clearly the Isaiah of the exile needed precisely the right

message in order to speak to the people's needs. In a situation like that, it is unlikely that we will have them unless we listen for them. The secret is to have a disciple's tongue, a mouth that speaks what the ears have learned. The teacher who knows how to sustain the weary is Yahweh himself. Yahweh is the one to give the right words to speak.

To have a disciple's tongue implies that, as a matter of principle and general character, the prophet has been committed to learning. Second Isaiah has been immersed in the words of the Torah, in the words of the prophets who lived before the exile, in the words of the Psalms. We know this is the case because their language is reflected in Second Isaiah's words. Isaiah of Jerusalem in particular had spoken of his own teaching being preserved among his disciples against the day when Israel would take it more seriously, and it is significant that the Second Isaiah here picks up the term that the First Isaiah had used. The later prophet sees himself as a disciple of the earlier one, called to follow his teaching and to become with him a disciple of Yahweh. Second Isaiah was a disciple of Yahweh in this general sense, a person who knew that no human message would do. It had to be what Yahweh taught.

Then Second Isaiah knew that this principle had to be applied day by day. Listening is a morning by morning activity. It is not, after all, so difficult to gain a general grasp of the truth, to know the Bible fairly well, to attain a fundamentally biblical theology. But to know what in particular needs to be said on a specific occasion is a very different matter. The Bible itself manifests considerable variety. Isaiah of Jerusalem says Yahweh is committed to Jerusalem and it will not fall; Jeremiah says Yahweh is not committed to Jerusalem and it will fall. Leviticus incorporates chapter after chapter about how to offer sacrifice, Amos says Yahweh is not really interested in sacrifice. Paul says the really important thing is faith, James says the really important thing is works. At different times the people of God need different things to be said to them. Thus the servant of God needs to be not only in a general sense a disciple of the

Lord, to acknowledge that the message must come from God, and to be well acquainted with the Scriptures. This principle has also to be applied from decade to decade, from year to year, and from day to day. It is easy to persist in declaring what was really God's word yesterday, but is inappropriate today because people are not in the same situation. As we have seen, this was characteristic of the false prophets in Israel. They were preaching yesterday's message, comforting people with words of prophecy that did not apply to them. An authentic prophet knows what Yahweh is saying today and is willing to confront people with it. School students listen to their teacher morning by morning. So it is also in Yahweh's school. The servant listens in order to be able to speak.

The servant is one who accepts affliction as the price of ministry

So "today's" message from Yahweh is one of comfort and encouragement for the exiles. The message is not as acceptable to the exiles as one might have thought. It was presumably even less acceptable to the Babylonians. Here is a prophet telling the wretched Jews that the Babylonians' enemy Cyrus is going to defeat Babylon. It will not be surprising if they feel compelled to do something about this dangerous person. So the price of being willing to bring God's word to the weary is to feel their enemies' rod on one's own back.

> The Lord Yahweh opened my ear,
> and I myself did not resist,
> I have not turned away.
> I yielded my back to flogging
> and my chin to those who tore at my beard.
> I did not hide my face
> from insults and spitting (50:5-6).

Piety in private (50:4) is backed up by courage in public, as the servant has had to face the fact that ministry brings trouble to the minister—as happened to Jeremiah. The picture here is reminiscent of that of Jesus, though the passage is not applied to him in the New Testament. The picture is also reminiscent of Paul. He, too, found that there was a cost involved in ministry, meeting with attack and persecution in many parts of the Mediterranean world where he was commissioned to spread the gospel (as he tells us in 2 Corinthians). He, too, accepts the affliction that comes to him, because he can see it has a positive purpose: "I am happy about my sufferings for you, for by means of my physical sufferings I am helping to complete what still remains of Christ's sufferings on behalf of his body, the church" (Col. 1:24 GNB).

In the same way, the Isaiah of the exile accepted what came to him: *I did not resist, I have not turned away. I yielded.... I did not hide....* The prophet knew it was all part of Yahweh's will. Having had a disciple's tongue, Second Isaiah had been declaring Yahweh's word, and could therefore take the consequences. The minister accepts affliction as the price of ministry. There is admittedly more to it than that, because somehow (as the story of Jeremiah hints, and as Paul recognizes) the acceptance of affliction achieves something. It speaks of the God who is willing to take pain and suffering, and it actually helps to bridge the gulf between God and people. But that becomes more explicit in Isaiah 53.

The servant is one who remains confident of Yahweh's vindication

> But the Lord Yahweh will help me.
> Thus I do not feel intimidated
> and have set my face like flint.
> I know I will not be disappointed.
> My Vindicator is near—who dares dispute with me?
> Let us confront one another.
> Who considers he has a case against me?
> Let him come forward.
> The Lord Yahweh will indeed help me:

> what man can put me in the wrong?
> They will indeed wear out like clothes,
> the moths will eat them up! (50:7-9).

The key factor in the situation is again Yahweh's word. It was Yahweh who gave the Isaiah of the exile that message about Cyrus defeating the Babylonians. The prophet could cope with their attacks on the basis of knowing that in the end they were doomed to fail.

How does the prophet expect to be vindicated? Will it be by Yahweh intervening in a trial at the hand of the Babylonians? Will it be by the fulfillment of the prophecies? Will the prophet's sufferings somehow convince people? (This idea appears in Isaiah 53). We do not know, and perhaps Second Isaiah did not know. Even a prophet only had the knowledge that Yahweh was faithful, not how Yahweh's faithfulness would be manifested.

We noted above a certain parallel between the experience of Paul and that of the servant prophet. Paul himself also takes up the theme of this passage and applies it to Christians generally. "If God is for us, who can be against us? ... Who will bring a charge against those whom God has chosen? It is God who justifies. Who is going to condemn?" So nothing can separate us from God's love (Rom. 8:31-39). God's servant can always be confident of God's vindication.

The servant's challenge

In giving this testimony, Second Isaiah has implicitly placed a choice before the hearers. Do the rest of the exiles intend to walk in the way of the servant, or in the way of the prophet's attackers? Two alternative and contrasting positions lie before them. The challenge becomes explicit in the verses that follow the servant's testimony (50:10-11). In a sense these are the climax towards which the testimony has been leading. It challenges them to walk the way of a disciple, not the way of an oppressor. The exiles stand between these alternatives.

> Who are there among you who revere Yahweh
> listen to the voice of his servant,
> who walks in darkness
> with no light to shine for him?
> They must trust in Yahweh
> and rely on their God (50:10).

Here the prophet is raising the flag for the formation of a faithful remnant. The idea of the remnant appears in several forms. The actual word has been used once or twice in these chapters. It was there when the prophet spoke about restoring the preserved of Israel, restoring what was left of Israel (49:6). That is the most basic thing that the idea means: the remnant is the people who are lucky enough to be left alive after Yahweh brings disaster. This remnant is not a group that is less sinful and rebellious than Israel in general. They are simply the ones who escaped the calamity. But that challenges them to become the remnant in an inward sense, the responsive, faithful remnant. This is the prophet's challenge. "You have heard me describing the life of a servant of God. God calls you to be willing to walk that way."

Second Isaiah also promises that it is the only worthwhile way, because the alternative is to slide into the way of the oppressor. That may be easier in the short run, but in the end it means being consumed by the fire you light. Yahweh declares where things will lead:

> But all you who are kindling a fire
> and surrounding yourself with sparks,
> walk in the flames of your fire
> and among the sparks you have lit.
> It is by my doing that this comes to you,
> so that you will lie down in torment (50:11).

CHAPTER TEN

The triumphant servant
Isaiah 52:13-53:12

After the challenge to respond to the servant's testimony (50:10), the servant motif again disappears for a while (51:1-52:11). The prophet continues to encourage the exiles' faith, directly and also indirectly—by exhorting Yahweh to act, as in 51:9-11. The servant motif is then developed quite markedly when it reappears (52:13-53:12: I refer to the passage loosely as "Isaiah 53"). Themes that have been present earlier are taken up and taken further.

The chapter as a whole is a deep and mysterious one. It is one of the most difficult passages in the Old Testament to translate into English—hence in part the differences between English translations. Many of the Hebrew words it uses are uncommon ones, the way the words fit together is often unclear, and (largely as a consequence of this) scholars have suspected that at various points the chapter has been altered by scribes, accidentally or purposefully, perhaps as a result of their own difficulty in understanding it. Yet it may be strangely appropriate that this deep and mysterious portrait of the suffering servant should be puzzling in many of its details. This helps to ensure that we do not make the mistake of thinking that we have totally grasped the picture it presents to us.

Indeed, I think "picture" or "vision" is the most helpful way to look at this chapter. We are familiar with visions related by Old Testament prophets. As we noted in chapter 3, Jeremiah once "saw" the world devastated as by a nuclear holocaust, a vision that spoke of the destruction hanging over Judah (see Jer. 4:23-28). Ezekiel relates a whole series of visions relating to the fall of Jerusalem and the coming restoration. In the New Testament, the book of Revelation presents itself substantially as one long vision (see Rev. 4:1). Again, some Christians today believe they are sometimes given a "picture" that expresses a message from God. In my experience, they avoid the word "vision," but the phenomenon is very similar. Our dreams, too, even if they are not supposed to have any religious significance, characteristically consist of a bewildering amalgam of images and memories from what has happened to us recently (or long ago) and from what has been on our minds.

So Isaiah 53 is a vision or a picture that addresses (sometimes obliquely, sometimes directly) the concerns of the prophet's ministry among the exiles, and reflects in different ways the prophet's own experience with the exiles and a subliminal acquaintance with various features of Israelite religion. This varied experience and knowledge contributes a range of motifs and images that combine to form something quite new and revolutionary, in the picture of a man afflicted but righteous, concerned to bring shalom to others and suffering for that, but ultimately triumphant and fruitful.

What the prophet actually sees

Second Isaiah pictures a man. He is not at all impressive.

> He grew straight up like a young plant
> with its roots in dry ground (53:2).

Healthy, fruitful plants, tall, strong trees, and beautiful, flourishing flowers grow only in well-watered ground. "A tree planted by streams of water… yields its fruit in its season, its leaf does not wither" (Ps. 1:3). But Israelites were familiar with the fact that as one travels south in their country, the land becomes drier and dustier and the trees become scarcer and more straggly, because they grow out of dry ground.

People, too, can be like that. This is true physically, as the pictures we see of undernourished children from starvation areas remind us. It is also true psychologically. People who have not been nourished emotionally or intellectually tend to grow up with their development of spirit, feelings or mind stunted. They are like plants with their roots in dry ground. This servant, too, reminded you of someone whose growth had been stunted.

Consequently there was nothing impressive or handsome about him. Nothing drew your attention to him. Now Jews do not have the negative attitude to physical appearances and material blessings that has often characterized the church. Their positive attitude goes back to a belief in God as the creator of the world and the Lord of material things. The Old Testament assumes that although God does look on the heart, nevertheless outward appearances matter; God is interested in them, too. Thus the Israelites expected their kings, for instance, to be six feet tall and stunningly handsome—and this is how Saul and David are described. "You are the most handsome of men," the king is told (Ps. 45:2). It is appropriate for him to be that.

But the man in the vision is not like this at all.

> He had no dignity or majesty to make us look at him.
> His appearance did not attract us to him (53:2).

Worse than that, he was a man *tormented by pain and humbled by suffering* (53:3). What kind of suffering? The prophet seems to refer both to physical illness and to persecution, and it is likely that we should not be too prosaic in utilizing every detail of the picture in order to form a composite whole—to prove he had one particular illness or had been attacked in one particular way. Yet we ought to take note of the various elements in the picture because they all contribute to the total effect of suffering and degradation.

Suffering tends to disfigure people. So it was with the man in the vision.

> He was disfigured, he no longer looked human.
> His appearance was no longer that of a man (52:14).

Sometimes a person or a photograph in a newspaper will make us shudder, and we may hear people say that such pictures of maimed or deformed people ought not to be put in the newspapers or on television. Such was the reaction aroused by the man in the vision. People were shocked and appalled at the sight of him. He himself knew this and had to live with it.

> He seemed vile, and avoided people,
> tormented by pain and humbled by suffering,
> like something men turn their faces from.
> He seemed vile, and we took no notice of him (53:3).

He knew what he looked like and he knew how people felt about him, so he avoided them and thereby in a sense saved himself the pain of rejection. For if he did come into contact with people, he found that no-one would look at him or acknowledge him. He was ignored, treated as if he did not exist. They could not cope with the sight except by ignoring it.

There was once a theory that what is actually being described here is a case of leprosy. Leprosy can eat away people's limbs and features, and one reason why the human instinct is to shut lepers away is that the sight is too much for people to cope with. It was the same with lunatics a century ago. It is unlikely that the prophet really has leprosy specifically in mind (and to complicate the picture, it is unlikely that the word translated "leprosy" in the Old Testament refers to what we mean by leprosy). But that suggestion gives the right impression: an appalling, disfiguring ailment that makes people instinctively recoil. Thus the man in the vision is without family or friends; he is alone. He is a social outcast.

That was a psychological reaction for people in the first

The triumphant servant

instance. But it became a theological principle. God had told Israel that there was generally a relationship between sin and suffering. Where relationships with God were right, there would be wholeness, growth, and health. When things went wrong between someone and God, one by-product would be that things went wrong in the person's other relationships (with the world, with nature, with society, with other people) and within the person. Yahweh would protect Israel from illness when things were right between it and God, but not when things were wrong.

So if they saw someone who was physically ill, for instance, it was at least a fair question whether things had gone wrong between the person and God. The story of Job, of course, makes it clear that this is not always the explanation, and many of the Psalms testify to this, too. But people easily slipped into the equation: sickness must imply sin. So they did with the man in this vision. In a sense what they were doing was rationalizing their instinctive rejection of him. They were providing a theological excuse for making him into a social outcast. Thus

> We for our part reckoned that he was afflicted,
> struck down by God, and brought low (53:4).

For the man in the vision, trouble then compounded itself. If people have made up their mind that someone is suffering so awfully that he must be an appalling sinner, then they may reckon it appropriate to treat him as an appalling sinner and to infer what sins he must have committed (as Job's "friends" did with Job). After all, the presence of sin in the community is not a mere private affair. It affects the whole people. It therefore has to be dealt with. Thus

> He was arrested and sentenced, and led away.
> And who gave a thought to his fate?
> Yes, he was torn from the world of the living (53:8).

He was condemned by society and counted among rebels

(53:12), included among those who threw off the laws of God and of the community. But then his status as a social outcast was reinforced and deepened. He was not even to receive an honorable burial. For an Old Testament believer, to die was to join your ancestors. You joined them physically in the family tomb. To be deprived of that last privilege is the final indignity, the final sadness and loss.

> He was given a grave among criminals,
> among the lowest of men at his death (53:9).

So what one actually saw in this man was a rather pathetic, underprivileged, unimpressive person; one who was disfigured by suffering and pain in such a way that he was shunned by people in general; one who was then assumed to be a marked transgressor and was treated as such, so that eventually he paid the ultimate penalty and was denied even family burial. But there was more to him than that.

What the prophet's insight perceives

There was something very puzzling about this man. The picture did not quite add up. He was thought to be a notorious sinner; that was assumed to be demonstrated by the suffering he had experienced. But when one looked at his reaction to the treatment he received when people had decided he was a wrongdoer, it did not fit. He did not react in the way you would expect of the notorious sinner he was supposed to be.

> He was harshly treated, though he submitted himself,
> he did not open his mouth,
> like a lamb led to the butcher's,
> like a sheep dumb before its shearers.
> He did not open his mouth (53:7).

Indeed, what wrong was he supposed to have done? He was *assumed* to be a gross sinner, but what was the evidence? When that question was asked, a strange contrast appeared between his

The triumphant servant

fate and the life he had actually lived.

> He was given a grave among criminals,
> among the lowest of men at his death,
> although he had done no wrong
> and his mouth had uttered no lie (53:9).

So why did he suffer the way he did? If he did not suffer affliction because he deserved it, was his suffering meaningless? Was there no explanation of it?

> Yet it was our suffering that he took,
> our pain he bore,
> whereas we had reckoned that he was afflicted,
> struck down by God, and brought low
> But he was wounded because of our rebellion,
> crushed because of our wrongdoing (53:4-5).

Why was this good man willing to be afflicted? One reason was that he wanted to identify with other people in their affliction.

To say he has borne our suffering does not in itself mean that he bore it *instead of us*. It can just mean that he bore it *with us*, when he did not have to. When Jews "sit shiva" with someone, they bear their grief and carry their sorrows, in the sense that they share them. That is something very valuable. One of the worst things about suffering is the feeling that you are alone, and it is some comfort to have someone to share your suffering with you. The man in the vision let himself be afflicted so that he could share the affliction that people in general brought on themselves by their sin.

But there is more to it than that. Here is this man who has done no wrong. He is a righteous man: that is Yahweh's own description (53:11). There was indeed a contrast between the man and the people who were watching him. But it was not, after all, that he was much more wicked than them. It was that he was much more righteous than them. He set a new standard of righteousness. After all, how many people manage to accept unfair treatment and hostile attacks in the way he does? How many people manage to control their words the way he did? Much later, James was to comment on what an uncontrollable fire the tongue is (James 3:6-9). Jesus declared that it was really unnecessary to worry about the kosher food laws because what actually defiles us is not what goes into our mouth but what comes out of it. No-one can be sinless as far as their words are concerned. But the man in the vision could keep his mouth shut (53:7). "Silence under Suffering is a strange thing in the Old Testament—a thing absolutely new.... In the Old Testament the sufferer is always either confessing his guilt to God, or, when he feels no guilt, challenging God in argument.... Why was this Servant the unique and solitary instance of silence under suffering?" (George Adam Smith, *The Book of Isaiah*, Volume 2, pp. 359-60).

Further, when he did open his mouth, he always spoke in accordance with the truth (53:9). Most strikingly, he "made intercession for the transgressors" (53:12 NRSV). There is more to this last line of the poem than that translation implies, as we shall suggest below, but the servant's attitude to those who afflict him at least includes this, that when he does open his mouth in the presence of those who are putting him to death for no reason, it is to pray for them. Who is this man?

In setting a new standard of righteousness, he makes people see themselves as sinners in a way they have not before. They started off feeling rather superior and upright when they compared themselves with him, but suddenly everything seemed to get turned upside down. As they looked more closely at him, they found that they had exchanged labels with him. He was supposed to be the sinner, they were the righteous. But as they continued to look at him, they found that he was the righteous one and they were the sinners. So he is suffering and they are not, whereas they are the sinners and he is not. Indeed *he* seems to be suffering for *their* sin, not merely in suffering alongside them, but in going through things that consequently they do not have to go through, even though he deserves those things much less than they do.

The triumphant servant

> He gave himself utterly, even to death,
> and let himself be counted among rebels.
> He took the sin of many
> and intervened for the rebels (53:12).

The point is made in a more technical way by speaking of his life as *offered for the guilt of others* (53:10). The prophet applies to him a term from the religious laws in Leviticus and Numbers, usually translated as "guilt-offering" (see Lev. 5–6). The prophet's acquaintance with these religious laws thus contributes one of the motifs that make up the eventual complex amalgam of his picture.

Now these laws included regulations for various types of sacrifice. Not all these sacrifices were centrally concerned with the problem of human sin and the barrier between humanity and God. Some were simply expressions of joyful fellowship or of gratefulness for answered prayer. But there were others that *were* indeed concerned with the problem of human sin. Regular "sin-offerings" (see Lev. 4) dealt with accidental religious offenses. On the annual Day of Atonement (see Lev. 16) the willful sins of the nation were transferred to a goat that was driven off into the wilderness. To us, such a ritual may seem only to heighten the problem: how can driving a goat into the wilderness deal with human sin? But somehow in Yahweh's providence it did. The other major kind of regular sacrifice concerned with sin was the "guilt-offering," to which Second Isaiah refers here. One particular function of this rite was to make restitution in connection with deliberate crimes such as robbery. Guilty people had to restore what they had stolen, but their offense was also a "breach of faith against Yahweh" (Lev. 6:2), and their act therefore had to be dealt with as a sin as well as a crime. The "guilt-offering" or "restitution-offering" was the means of getting right with Yahweh in such a situation of deliberate sin. The servant's life is offered on behalf of sinners in the way that an animal's life is offered according to this rite.

Israelite religious law had no place for human sacrifice. The

Israelites were aware of this practice, but they knew it as a Canaanite one, into which Israel fell only in times of apostasy. Long before the time of Moses, their forefather Abraham had come close to offering Isaac his son as a human sacrifice to God, but he had then been told that this was not required (see Gen. 22). God valued Abraham's willingness to yield up the one most dear to him, the one whom God had designed as the means by which to fulfill the promise to Abraham. But the actual doing of the act was prohibited. God provided a goat instead.

On the other hand, the possibility of one righteous person giving their life to secure the lives of a sinful people had been raised before in Israel's history. We referred in chapter 2 to Moses' desire to give up his own life if Yahweh's anger was to burn up the Israelites (see Exod. 32:30-32). In the opening chapter of Deuteronomy, Moses speaks of himself as forbidden to enter the promised land because of Yahweh's anger, not with him but with the Israelite people (Deut. 1:37). The idea of Moses being punished for the sins of the people is another thread in the tapestry that the prophet is weaving. In a sense, the servant is a new Moses. He is thus not a dumb animal, led to the butcher's uncomplaining because it does not recognize the place (53:7). He is not even, like Isaac, led off to Mount Moriah to be offered to God because his father thinks it is a good idea. Like Moses, the man in the vision offers himself. As a mature adult he faces up to the need of a sacrifice and agrees to be the sacrifice.

The necessity of sacrifice presupposes the breakdown of relationship between Israel and God. The achievement of the servant's affliction is to restore that relationship, and to restore the wholeness that depends upon it.

> The chastening that brings us "shalom" was required of him
> and through his wounds healing came to us (53:5).

Some time ago the prophet lamented Israel's loss of *shalom* and declared that rebels (like Israel) could never find it again (48:18, 22). It is rediscovered through someone being chastened on its

The triumphant servant

behalf. Way back at the beginning of the book of Isaiah, Israel is a sick man, bruised and beaten because of his rebelliousness (1:5-6). Healing comes through someone being wounded on his behalf.

The servant willingly accepted what came to him for the sake of these who needed to be brought back to God. But the prophet also perceives that Yahweh was involved. *Yahweh has brought down on him the guilt that belonged to all of us* (53:6). Yahweh was involved in the career of that unexpected anointed one, Cyrus, through whom the people were to be brought back to Judah, and had said about him, *he will fulfill my whole plan* (44:28). Yahweh is involved also in the career (or the anti-career) of this unnamed servant, through whom wholeness is to be restored to all those who acknowledge him. Indeed, the prophet says about him, *it was Yahweh's plan to crush him with pain* (53:10). As in the case of Cyrus, this involves no overriding of the human will: he willingly accepts the role Yahweh has in mind for him, and thereby his will and Yahweh's will coincide.

His life thus reveals something of Yahweh's own power. This is where the witnesses' testimony began.

> Who would have believed what we have heard?
> To whom has Yahweh's power manifested itself? (53:1).

We are familiar with the idea of the power of Yahweh (more literally, the "arm" of Yahweh). What it suggests is made clear only a few verses before this vision of the suffering servant: "Yahweh has bared his holy arm before the eyes of all the nations, and all the ends of the earth will see our God act to save us" (52:10). Yahweh's arm raised in violent action against his enemies is a characteristic Old Testament motif. But here in the vision of the servant is a very different understanding of the arm of Yahweh. "Who could have seen the LORD's hand in this" (53:1 GNB), in the affliction and humiliation of this servant? Strange power of God, manifested in such weakness.

Thus the prophet's insight perceives that the man who was afflicted did not behave like a wrongdoer. So why was he suffering? To share the experience of those who do suffer. But then, looking at him more closely, the prophet sees that he is afflicted more severely than others, even though he deserves it much less than others (in fact, not at all). One look at the servant makes it clear that they are the sinners, not he. He is in fact suffering in their place, in the way an animal does when it is offered in sacrifice. And the whole thing is somehow Yahweh's own idea, and it reveals something very deep about Yahweh and about where Yahweh's real might lies.

What the prophet ultimately looks for

The servant *gave himself utterly, even to death* (53:12). So is there any future for him?

> When his life is offered for the guilt of others,
> He will see his offspring and enjoy long life (53:10).

His suffering is not to be the end of him. He is to enjoy a full life, despite the death he seems to have died. What does an Old Testament man look for from a full life? He hopes to beget many sons, so that his quiver is full of them (Ps. 127:5), and to live to a good old age, to be full of years (Gen. 25:8). Despite what he has been through, *he will see his offspring and enjoy long life,* the witnesses declare. He was involved in Yahweh's purpose and Yahweh will see justice is done.

But one doubts if a man like this was very concerned for his own future. He had surrendered himself to the needs of sinful people and to the purpose of Yahweh. His concern will be, what about those needs? What about that purpose? He is promised that the purpose will be achieved and the needs will be met. It will not all be useless.

> Through him Yahweh's purpose will prosper.
> He will see fruit from his deep affliction,
> He will find satisfaction through his humiliation.
> My servant, being righteous, will bring righteousness to many.
> He will bear their guilt himself (53:10-11).

The triumphant servant

Early on in the exposition of the servant motif, the bringing of God's just government to the weak and needy emerged as a significant feature in the servant calling (see 42:1-4). Yahweh's servant is involved in the fulfilling of Yahweh's righteous purpose (42:6). The servant is now promised the satisfaction of knowing that his affliction does not ruin that purpose: his humiliation bears fruit in bringing righteousness to many. At the beginning of the poem Yahweh promises,

> My servant will succeed (52:13).

At the end, Yahweh promises that his achievement will be acknowledged and rewarded.

> I will give him many as his possession
> and he will distribute the mighty as spoil (53:12).

Indeed, the way his success is to be acknowledged perhaps implies something more than the honor of a great man.

> He will rise to greatness and high honor (52:13).

The words recall those of Isaiah of Jerusalem at the beginning of his ministry, when he saw his vision of Yahweh the holy one in his temple, "high and exalted" (6:1). It is the same words that are used of the servant in this vision, near the end of the book of Isaiah. He receives "a share in the dignity of Yahweh himself" (D. R. Jones, in *Peake's Commentary on the Bible*, p. 527). Mysteriously, the power of God was manifested in his humiliation (53:1) and mysteriously, the glory of God is reflected in his triumph.

Thus, whereas people have been appalled at the sight of the servant in his disfigurement, now they will rise to their feet to acknowledge him in his triumph. Whereas people once derided him, then they will be speechless at the sight of him in his moment of success. Then they will acknowledge that they have seen something quite unprecedented and unique, something they had never dreamt of, something no-one could have believed or seen the significance of. But they will at last perceive it.

> He will bring many nations to their feet
> and kings will stand speechless before him,
> because they have seen something they have not been told
> before,
> and contemplated something they have not heard of before
> (52:15).

What the prophet ultimately looks for is the servant's vindication. He seems to be finished, but he will live a long and happy life yet. His suffering was not pointless; it will bring release to many. His humiliation was not permanent; he will receive a share in God's own exaltation. He will not be despised for ever, but acknowledged by nations and kings. Ordinary sight sees only the affliction. But the eyes of faith see the meaning behind it, and the eyes of hope see the fruit that is to issue from it.

Who is this man?

I noted at the beginning of the chapter that many of the details of the prophet's portrayal of the servant in Isaiah 53 are difficult to interpret though the overall picture is clear enough. The mystery that has most preoccupied readers, however, is the question who is the servant in the prophet's vision.

What might have been the answer if we had been able to ask the prophet the question? I suspect that Second Isaiah's first response would have been to say, "Well, I have told you all I know. It is there in the book. I have nothing else to tell you. If I had, I would have put it in."

But then if we pressed the question, "How is the vision going to come true?", there are two things he might have said. One is this. "I have been describing to you, or expressing in this vision, certain insights that I have come to about how God is going to win Israel back, and how God is going to bring light to the world. I know from the Torah, for instance, that God speaks of sacrifice being necessary if sin is to be atoned for. I know from

The triumphant servant

what Israel has gone through and from what Yahweh has promised with regard to its future, that it is possible for affliction to be followed by triumph and for death to be followed by resurrection. I know from my own experience as a prophet that bringing people back to God often demands a personal cost, a personal self-giving, a personal dying on the part of the one who is involved in ministry. So in a sense what I have been describing in this vision is what needs to happen if the deepest problem between Israel and God is to be dealt with. I do not know how it is going to be achieved. But that is what does need to be achieved."

"But that is really too tentative a way to put it. It might suggest that I am only saying what needs to happen, but have no conviction that it ever will happen. That is not what I mean. God gave me my vision. It is about God's purpose for the world. It is about what God promises to bring about. So it is not just my pious hope. It is God's promise. But how he is going to keep his promise—well, I do not know about that."

So has the vision found its realization? Jewish interpretation of Isaiah 53 has naturally been struck by the parallels between the portrait of the servant and the experience of the Jewish people. Indeed, Isaiah of Jerusalem himself described the suffering of Israel (more accurately, of Judah) in these terms, in a passage referred to above.

> Your head is covered with sores,
> your body diseased;
> from head to foot there is not a sound spot in you—
> nothing but bruises and weals and raw wounds
> that have not felt compress or bandage or soothing oil.

Isaiah goes on to make it quite clear that the portrait of the sick man is a metaphorical description of the nation:

> Your country is desolate, your cities lie in ashes.
> Strangers devour your land before your eyes (1:5-7 NEB).

That earlier passage from Isaiah at least makes it clear that the fact that the picture in Isaiah 53 is a picture of an individual man does not mean that the servant referred to needs be an individual—the Messiah to come, or the prophet, or a contemporary such as the exiled and imprisoned King Jehoiachin (though the suffering of the prophet and that of the king in exile may have contributed to the picture). The nation as a whole is like a sick man, who eventually (with the exile) actually dies. But death need not be the end. "Can these bones live again?" Yahweh asks Ezekiel. Ezekiel wisely declines to express an opinion, but Yahweh says to the bones, "I will put muscles on you, I will bring flesh on you, I will cover you with skin, and I will put breath in you, and you will come to life" (Ezek. 37:3-6). Israel before the exile was a sick man and Israel in the exile is a corpse, but Yahweh promises to restore it to life.

Often since that time Israel has suffered in the way the servant did. Often its suffering has been relatively undeserved. Sometimes its suffering has borne fruit for others: the death of the six million might make it unlikely that the world will tolerate another Hitler (as D. N. Freedman suggests in an article on "The Biblical Idea of History" in *Interpretation* 21, 1967, p. 48). The trouble is that the world has a short memory. Again, would the State of Israel have been founded except for the West's need to salve its conscience for the holocaust? The trouble is that even the State of Israel may not be safe. The Jewish novelist Saul Bellow relates in his diary of a four month stay in Israel, *To Jerusalem and Back* (p. 15), "A Jewish professor at Harvard recently said to me, 'Wouldn't it be the most horrible of ironies if the Jews had collected themselves conveniently in one country for a second holocaust?'."

Israel's own story does illustrate aspects of the vision of the suffering servant. But in other respects it does not quite fit. We have already seen that in the prophet's view Israel as much as the nations is rebellious instead of righteous, and itself needs to find *shalom*. Like the church, it needs the ministry of the servant, who is (unlike it) righteous, uncomplaining, unvengeful,

The triumphant servant

undeceiving, and praying for his persecutors, before it can function as God's servant itself. The actual text of the passage may even make explicit that the servant and the people are to be distinguished, by drawing a comparison between their sufferings:

> As many were appalled by you (my people, NEB adds),
> so he was disfigured... (52:14).

But certainly Israel's suffering contributes something to the prophet's vision; to be the servant is Israel's calling, to suffer like the servant has been its experience, and it is distasteful for a gentile to attempt to disallow it to find itself in this passage.

Nevertheless the Christian's testimony is that there is one particular Jew who has lived up to the portrait offered by the vision of Isaiah 53, and that is Jesus of Nazareth. The New Testament picks up many of the specific phrases of the chapter to apply them to Jesus. His life manifested no sin or untruth (1 Peter 2:22, compare Isa. 53:9). His ministry took many people's suffering and pain (Matt. 8:17, compare Isa. 53:4). His mission met with disbelief (John 12:37-38, compare Isa. 53:4). He accepted oppression without protest (Acts 8: 32-33, compare Isa. 53:7-8). He let himself be taken as a criminal (Luke 22:37, compare Isa. 53:12). He died to bear people's sins, to heal people's wounds, to restore straying sheep to their shepherd (1 Peter 2:24-25, compare Isa. 53:5-6). The conviction that Jesus fulfills the vision of the servant of Yahweh lies behind other passages where reference to Isaiah 53 is more allusive:

> Of his own free will he gave up all he had,
> and took the nature of a servant....
> He was humble and walked the path of obedience all the way
>   to death—
> his death on the cross.
> For this reason God raised him to the highest place above
> and gave him the name that is greater than any other name
> (Phil. 2:7-9 GNB).

Jesus is the suffering and triumphant servant par excellence.

To see Jesus as the fulfillment of this vision in Isaiah 53 brings home to us two aspects of his ministry. One is that he suffers to effect atonement between God and humanity. "God was in Christ..."; the suffering of Jesus is the suffering of the crucified God, letting people do their worst so as to make an end to their sin once and for all by absorbing all the hostility and aggression they can express. Humanity's fundamental problem is sin; the starting-point of Jesus' proclamation is his very Jewish call for repentance or turning from sin (Mark 1:15), and the culmination of his work is his dying for sin.

But often people's felt problem is not their sin but their pain and suffering; and what often actually drew people to Jesus was his concern for and his ability to deal with such needs. Many parts of the church have experienced a new realization of this in the widespread concern with healing—indeed, there is once again a danger of a loss of perspective, of forgetting that sin and atonement remain the fundamental matters. But as long as we see that our need of forgiveness remains our deepest need, we can go on to rejoice that because Jesus died for us the rest of our ills can be dealt with precisely because sin, atonement, and forgiveness are the root matters. We can bring our sins to the cross and leave them there; we can also bring our pains, our griefs, and our sorrows to the cross and leave them there. We need not hang on to them. The servant suffers both for our rebellion and for our pain and suffering.

It is striking, however, that when the epistles in the New Testament speak of Jesus in these terms, the context is concerned not merely with a right understanding of Jesus, but with his followers' willingness to walk the way Jesus walked. "Christ... left you an example, so that you might follow in his steps" (1 Peter 2:21); "the attitude you should have is the one Christ Jesus had" (Phil. 2:5 GNB). The danger of the quest for the identity of the servant in Isaiah 53 is that it diverts us from the same challenge that the chapter lays before us. The poem offers a vision of what God wants to do and can do with

The triumphant servant

someone prepared to be a servant. The poem is, to use a more prosaic term, a job-description. Or it is a challenge to readers regarding whether they are prepared to be a servant of this kind. The challenge, or invitation, may be accepted by Israel as a nation or by the church or by individuals who are willing to take it seriously. While Christians are convinced that Jesus alone met the challenge in the fullest sense, this does not mean that the passage is now a dead thing from the past, relevant only as a promise fulfilled in Christ. It is still God's vision for people, and God's challenge to us.

> The poem... exists to create another world, a world indeed that is recognizably our own, with brutality and suffering and God and a coming-to-see on the part of some, but not a world that simply once existed and is gone for good.... The poem can become true in a variety of circumstances.... The world which the poem creates is a topsy-turvy world when judged by ordinary human standards.... The social order, the strength of numbers, good taste, ordinary human decency, and the justice of God are all in turn called into question by this topsy-turvy, not to say shocking, poem. This is the world that the reader is bidden to give his assent to—or rather, to enter. It is not an obviously appealing invitation (David J. A. Clines, *I, He, We, and They: A Literary Approach to Isaiah 53*, pp. 61-62).

So the vision challenges us, too, as to whether we are prepared to look at our ministry the way this passage looks at the servant's. Consider what is involved. All one can actually see is disfigurement, suffering, pain, loss, abandonment, misunderstanding, and death. That is all that is visible. But then we are challenged to look with the insight of faith and see that the suffering, the pain, and the loss can be mysteriously meaningful and mysteriously glorious. But one cannot physically see this. One can see it only with the eyes of faith. We are further challenged to look with the foresight of hope, and see that the abandonment, misunderstanding, and death will not be final; they will yet bear fruit and bring freedom to people. But one cannot see it now. One can see it only with the eyes of hope. That is the vision's challenge to our lives and our ministry.

> The force of the poem is not simply to invite the reader to approximate his behavior and lifestyle to that of the servant as best he can; it is rather that the figure of the servant seizes, imposes itself upon a reader.... The assumption of the servant's role becomes, not the voluntary act of a dramatic role-playing, but a compulsion by the figure of the servant (Clines, p. 64).

That being the case, what I want to leave the reader with is not my reflections on the suffering servant, but the suffering servant himself. Arguably, the place for the "text" in a sermon is not the beginning (after which it can be abandoned for the preacher's own thoughts) but the end, after it has been, one hopes, a little elucidated. (I owe this point to a paper by David Clines, "Notes for an Old Testament Hermeneutic," *Theology, News and Notes* 21, 1975, p. 10). So what does Isaiah 53 do to you?

> My servant will succeed,
> he will rise to greatness and high honor.
> As many were appalled at you,
> so he was disfigured, he no longer looked human.
> His appearance was no longer that of a man.
> So he will bring many nations to their feet
> and kings will stand speechless before him,
> because they have seen something they have not been told before,
> and contemplated something they have not heard of before.
> Who would have believed what we have heard?
> To whom has Yahweh's power manifested itself?
> He grew straight up like a young plant
> with its roots in dry ground.
> He had no dignity or majesty to make us look at him.
> His appearance did not attract us to him.
> He seemed vile, and avoided people,
> tormented by pain and humbled by suffering,
> like something people turn their faces from.

The triumphant servant

He seemed vile, and we took no notice of him.
Yet it was our suffering that he took,
our pain he bore,
whereas we for our part reckoned that he was afflicted,
struck down by God, and brought low.
But he was wounded because of our rebellion,
crushed because of our wrongdoing.
The chastening that brings us "shalom" was required of him
and through his wounds healing came to us.
All of us have strayed like sheep,
we have each of us taken his own way,
but Yahweh has brought down on him
the guilt that belonged to all of us.
He was harshly treated, though he submitted humbly,
he did not open his mouth,
like a lamb led to the butcher's,
like a sheep dumb before its shearers.
He did not open his mouth.
He was arrested and sentenced, and led away,
and who gave a thought to his fate?
Yes, he was torn from the world of the living
because of the rebellion of my people, who deserved the
    affliction.
He was given a grave among criminals,
among the lowest of people at his death,
although he had done no wrong,
and his mouth had uttered no lie.
But it was Yahweh's plan to crush him with pain.
When his life is offered for the guilt of others,
he will see his offspring and enjoy long life
and through him Yahweh's plan will prosper.
He will see fruit from his deep affliction,
he will find satisfaction through his humiliation.
My servant, being righteous, will bring righteousness to many,
he will bear their guilt himself.
Therefore I will give him many as his possession
and he will distribute the mighty as spoil,

because he gave himself utterly, even to death,
and let himself be counted among rebels.
He took the sin of many
and intervened for the rebels.

If you have ears to hear, then hear.

www.ingramcontent.com/pod-product-compliance
Lightning Source LLC
Chambersburg PA
CBHW072138160426
43197CB00012B/2154